The Crisis in Forecasting and the Emergence of the "Prospective" Approach
(Pergamon Policy Studies-15)

Pergamon Titles of Related Interest

Barney   *The Global 2000 Report to the President of the U.S.: Entering the 21st Century*

Brown   *Disaster Preparedness and the United Nations: Advance Planning for Disaster Relief*

Demir   *Arab Development Funds in the Middle East*

Graham/Jordan   *The Changing Role and Concept of the International Civil Service*

Laszlo/Baker/Eisenberg/Raman   *The Objectives of the New International Economic Order*

Lozoya/Estevez/Green et al.   *Alternative Views of the New International Economic Order: A Survey and Analysis of Major Academic Research Reports*

Perry/Kraemer   *Technological Innovations in American Local Governments: The Case of Computing*

Renninger   *Multinational Cooperation for Development in West Africa*

Singh/Titli   *Systems: Decomposition, Optimisation and Control*

PERGAMON
POLICY
STUDIES

The Crisis in Forecasting and the Emergence of the "Prospective" Approach

With Case Studies in Energy and Air Transport

Michel Godet

Translated by
J.D. Pearse
Harry K. Lennon

Published for UNITAR

Pergamon Press

NEW YORK • OXFORD • TORONTO • SYDNEY • FRANKFURT • PARIS

Pergamon Press Offices:

U.S.A.   Pergamon Press Inc., Maxwell House, Fairview Park, Elmsford, New York 10523, U.S.A.

U.K.   Pergamon Press Ltd., Headington Hill Hall, Oxford OX3 0BW, England

CANADA   Pergamon of Canada, Ltd., 150 Consumers Road, Willowdale, Ontario M2J, 1P9, Canada

AUSTRALIA   Pergamon Press (Aust) Pty. Ltd., P O Box 544, Potts Point, NSW 2011, Australia

FRANCE   Pergamon Press SARL, 24 rue des Ecoles, 75240 Paris, Cedex 05, France

FEDERAL REPUBLIC   Pergamon Press GmbH, 6242 Kronberg/Taunus,
OF GERMANY   Pferdstrasse 1, Federal Republic of Germany

Originally published as <u>Crise de la Prevision—Essor de la Prospective</u> par Michel Godet, © 1977 Presses Universitaires de France.

Copyright © 1979 Pergamon Press Inc.

Library of Congress Cataloging in Publication Data

Godet, Michel, 1948-
    The crisis in forecasting and the emergence of the "prospective" approach.

    (Pergamon policy studies)
    Translation of Crise de la prevision, essor de la prospective.
    Bibliography: p.
    Includes index.
    1. Economic forecasting. I. Title.
HB3730.G5613   1978   330'.07'23   78-10548

Printed in the United States of America

Contents

Foreword

Michel Godet's book could not have come at a more appropriate time. It is highly relevant to the immediate preoccupations of the United Nations, as the organization braces for the advent of a new decade, laying the groundwork for one of the periodic "grand designs" that sustain the pulse of institutions. For an observer standing at the periphery of the international system, a new type of malaise is discernible, more so perhaps than for those engaged in the relentless process of negotiation. This feeling does not just come today, as so often in the past, from a lagging political will, as governments move from one forum to another in the elusive quest for binding commitments. Its source may rather be found in a widespread conceptual disarray as the validity of traditional modes of thinking and the policies informed by them are increasingly called into question.

Current situations, when submitted to analytical scrutiny, reveal complexities as well as discontinuities that were not formerly present, or not taken into account. They tax the predictive and planning capacity of policy-makers. There are also anticipatory or speculative ideas that seem to develop somewhat autonomously around the great debate on "the future," but may have an impact on the decision-makers.

The most conspicuous - but by no means the most important - element contributing to the present state of mind and the related problems of interpretation is probably the petroleum syndrome. It can obviously be seen as a discontinuity, since the pattern of price relationship and external balances on which all economic projections were based is significantly altered. But it is now clear that the adaptability of the international system to the phenomenon was misjudged. Scenarios of catastrophe have of late made more waves than scenarios of resilience. It therefore came as a surprise to many that the much advertised "energy crunch" is not materializing and that the international financial system is resisting the shock, albeit not without annoyances.

Gloomy predictions, popular in the early 1970s, have also combined with the effects of a severe and prolonged recession to propagate the view, now widely shared, although not convincingly documented, of a break in the historical growth trends in the industrial world, foreshadowing an era of slow advance with its inevitable impact on the economics of developing countries. There may be here the making of a self-fulfilling prophecy, constricting the policy options of those politicians who look beyond the management of the short-term cycle.

But it is, above all, the universal exigency of social change that·confounds and defeats our customary analytical approaches; these are based on a very partial understanding of the mechanisms through which societies evolve, and are better geared to scenarios of "reproduction" than of "transformation."

The persistence of mass poverty in the Third World cannot indefinitely be ascribed to insufficient efforts, national or international, without the question of their direction being raised.   As attention focuses on the satisfaction of basic needs, rather than on growth of the aggregate product, governments often acknowledge the need for a change in their course of action. But doubts arise in regard to policies that have not passed the test of experimentation and are not articulated within a satisfactory analytical framework.

The conceptual embarrassment is no less conspicuous in the industrial countries. During the recent election campaign in France it was not possible for the opposition to project a credible program of social transformation, even as a change in the political setup appeared desirable to a majority of the electorate.   The mechanisms likely to lead, in the context of mixed economics and parliamentary democracies, to more justice and sustained employment, are not as yet adequately defined. As a result, the political discourse, unfolding traditional themes, seemed divorced from a probably new sociological situation. Following successive economic miracles, with widespread and spectacular improvement in the lot of the workers and the provision of collective services, the process of continuing progress may now have derailed on a hard core of stubborn poverty. The political class can overlook the poverty, which is larger than usually recognized, because it is compounded by the existence of ethnic minorities largely confined to ghettos and of migrant labor without ready access to the political arena or the powerful unions that determine the course of labor negotiation. Indeed, one may well wonder whether there is not, after all, and in spite of so many triumphant declarations to the contrary, a phenomenon of pauperization inherent in the present structure of industrial societies. But it remains outside the confines of the political chessboard where various factions of a majority, either benefiting from the system, or hoping to benefit from it in the near future, compete in a sometimes fierce confrontation, against a backdrop of unconscious and unacknowledged complicity.

When seeking to promote social change, all governments, more often than not, are confronted with the "counterintuitive" effects that J. W. Forrester* of the Massachusetts Institute of Technology identified in relation to the dynamics of urban problems.   Situations exhibit this "counterintuitive" characteristic of course only when the problems are not correctly formulated and the context of interactions is not well understood; but this is bound to occur in complex situations where it is not possible to change one factor without interfering with a host of others.   The absence of a theoretical

---

* "Urban Dynamics," 1969

framework attuned to such circumstances is one of the features of the contemporary problematique.

The dominant paradigm that inspired the policies of international cooperation was derived from neoclassical theories of growth and equilibrium, to be achieved through market mechanisms, subject to some minimum regulation and with the corrective for developing countries of induced or organized transfers of capital and technology. The paradigm was never more than vaguely formulated; it harbored from the beginning, and gathered on the way, a not inconsiderable number of deviations that should have induced skepticism as to the strength of its theoretical foundations. But it conferred legitimacy to policies that might be called "pragmatic-functional," and it was translated in the creation of institutions and the adoption of nonbinding rules of international conduct. Above all, it derived its validation from a set of favorable circumstances that prevailed for more than a quarter century.

The neoclassical paradigm was not the only one to claim the allegiance of the international community; it had to compete with others. They did not, however, enjoy such a wide field of influence: the "Marxist" model, and later the "dependencia" model so important in Latin American parlance, and, even more recently, an incipient "ecological" model.

None of these or other paradigms may be said to proceed from an integrative theory that would provide a reliable holistic view, a coherent representation covering a significant part of a complex social reality and facilitating the consensus among a large section of the intelligentsia and the body politic. Yet, provided they are not deceptively applied to the analysis of whole systems, they may still assist in the explanatory and exploratory processes, as segments or fragments of theories. It is dangerous for instance to pursue normative policies without any reference to equilibrium theories, if only to identify the margins of freedom and the costs of transgressing them. It is equally fallacious to chart an evolutive or reformist path while overlooking, as in so many of the more prominent future studies, the inherent conflicts of groups or classes and the reality of unequal exchange. The "dependencia" paradigm, perhaps more pertinent to the analysis of the past than to the shaping of the future, can still be useful as a mobilizing concept, and it brings an important dimension to the elucidation and probing of outward-oriented versus self-reliant policies. Under the uncertainties revealed but not dissolved by the early reports of the Club of Rome, the "ecological" model - with its attention to diminishing returns, its discriminatory approach to technology, and its valuable concept of "care and maintenance" - may give important clues to a better management of small or large social systems.

Still, compared with other periods, society must operate today within a fragmented conceptual framework. This situation must be recognized and accepted. While we are now aware of the limited usefulness of old paradigms, we have not as yet acquired enough empirical knowledge on which to base the construction of new ones. The attempt to do so might even be as misleading and paralyzing as the continuing adherence to obsolescent models. It is in this context, largely forced upon us by new perceptions and the expansion of our cognitive powers, that the present more modest ambition to forge new methodological tools applicable to the analysis of specific situations and problems must be viewed. Within this promising movement the "prospective" approach occupies a special place and exhibits distinct advantages. Initiated in France by Gaston Berger and Bertrand de Jouvenel, it has become an important tool in the double task, inherent in all "futures" studies, of discovering the consistency of multiple objectives and exploring the path leading to their most desirable combinations. "Prospective" (the word is new also in the French language) is open to a great diversity of interpretations and supports many creative enterprises. A certain philosophical background is common to all of them: a refusal to see the future as unique and determined. The importance, repeatedly underlined by Michel Godet, of "desire" or "wish fulfillment" as a productive force indicates - more explicitly than with any other approach to futures studies - that the very essence of "prospective" lies in the twilight zone where determinism and freedom are locked in their everlasting dialectical contest. It follows that some of the most important elements affecting the dynamics of social systems are the nonmeasurable ones. Indeed the appropriate linking of political and cultural factors with the study of such phenomena as inflation, investment, distribution, or consumption patterns has become one of the major unsolved problems of mathematical modeling. Beyond the qualitative scenario analysis that characterized its early manifestations, "prospective" is now more and more enriched and strengthened by the use of methods flexibly adapted from the natural sciences. Michel Godet aptly describes them and shows how they can be simultaneously or sequentially combined within some kind of synthesis.

"Prospective" also increasingly relates to other forms of reflection on the future. It would be wrong to view it as antinomic with mathematical modeling, which became the privileged tool in the early phase of the "futures" movement. Its limitations have by now been well accounted for. Nevertheless, there is little doubt that it will become a major and more reliable instrument of short- and long-term planning, as the empirical data base is improved and as the development of discriminant statistical analysis helps in the discovery of correlations and regularities. Factors that today remain external to the mathematical models, particularly the nonmeasurable ones, may be gradually absorbed within their structures. Even in the present state of the art, mathematical models may be seen as useful control mechanisms in certain phases of the scenario analysis developed by the "prospective" approach, and their results may in turn generate new ideas and opportunities for scenario analysis.

In a world where so many disciplines must contribute to our understanding of the social reality, the "prospective" approach will also be seen as having close affinities with the research pursued within the modern historical school, to which French historians such as Braudel and Leroy-Ladurie have made distinctive contributions. In the definition of the paths leading to social change, an understanding of the different layers of historic evolution, the coexistence over long periods of social structures inherited from the past or pointing to the future may provide important insights into the strategic areas where normative policies can be successfully applied.

Because it starts from "images of the future," multiple by definition, "prospective" is especially relevant to the problems of international society. The world community is so unstructured, even amorphous, it is not unreasonable to surmise that the spectrum of its possible futures is wider than in the case of other situations. One intuitively senses that the present period is an important crossroads. Directions and orientations are not wholly determined, but they may be fateful in the sense that they would be difficult to reverse if they prove to be the wrong choices. This may be the case with decisions on trade and finance affecting the very fabric of international economic intercourse, or with the geopolitical consequences of a prolonged incapacity to promote social change, or the failure to bring under control the more ambivalent products of new science and technology.

This is why Michel Godet's book has a practical value that matches its epistemological contribution. Because his reflection is rooted in a vast culture and set within a broad philosophical context, he can discuss in exact and technical terms - and apply to concrete cases - promising methodological instruments, which he himself has helped to develop, while placing them in a perspective whose larger significance can hardly escape the reader.

Philippe de Seynes

La Prospective (French) Science which studies the technical, scientific, economic and social forces making for accelerated change and attempts to predict the kinds of situations which could result from their interplay... La Prospective, according to its first proponent, G. Berger, is neither a doctrine, nor a system. It is a way of focusing and concentrating on the future by imagining it full-blown rather than by drawing deductions from the present.

Translated from Grand Larousse, 1963 edition.

I

Toward Global, Qualitative, and Multiple Forecasting of an Uncertain Future: The Prospective Approach

1 Introduction—The Prospective: Man Creates the Future

Our century is one of change, uncertainty, and action. Acceleration in the pace of change contributes to uncertainty about the future and thus makes assumptions about the future necessary to guide our present actions.

History is influenced by the attitudes of men toward the future; as their outlook changes, so does their anticipation of future events. Passive, adaptive, and activist attitudes toward the future have been reflected historically in the different stages through which predicting and forecasting the future - and the perception of them - have passed: forecasting as a contingent activity, forecasting as an essential activity, and forecasting as a flawed activity.

The inadequacy of forecasting techniques can be measured by the numerous errors they have led to, explained by the systematic elimination of the part played by creative human action in determining the future. This creative attitude is recognized by the "prospective" approach, which reflects awareness of a future that is both deterministic and free, both passively suffered and actively willed.

THE STAGES OF FORECASTING

We shall distinguish between the stages of forecasting as a contingent activity, as an essential activity, and as a flawed activity.

Forecasting as a Contingent Concept

The concept of a future, or the possibility of anticipating it, has not always existed. It was the Indo-European languages that first gave verbal form to the idea of a future.

Prediction is a relative concept that depends on the period and society

3

that employs it.   Until the industrial revolution, forecasting was un-
necessary.   Indeed, the word "future" did not appear in Diderot's Encyclo-
pédie, (1751-1752).   Even more significant, the word "forecasting" is not
mentioned once in Henri Denis' index of history and economic thought (14),
and the word "prospective" does not appear in the chapter dealing with
forecasting in the dictionary of economic science published in 1958. (15)
Anticipating the future in earlier times was part of prediction and prophecy,
i.e., revelation.   Thus Richelet's dictionary of 1739 defines prediction:
"theological term; used of God and means knowledge of what will come." (24)
Used in this sense, the future is conceived as something that bears the same
relation to the present as the present bears to the past. From there it is no
great step to imagine that there is only one single, predetermined form the
future can take, just as there is only a single past, since everything is
preordained by God.

This kind of forecasting/predicting does not conceive of the impact of
human actions on events since it looks at the world fatalistically. Confronted
with his inevitable future, man adopts a passive attitude. He submits to his
destiny. What is the use of thinking about the future? Why complicate the
present with worries of future disasters? Tomorrow will be tomorrow and
there is nothing to be done about it. Prediction, even when it exists, is not
necessary because the world changes slowly, and tomorrow will be like today
in the same way that today was like yesterday. This passive attitude toward
the future and the contingent form of forecasting still persist in most slowly
changing societies. In industrial countries, on the other hand, the decline of
religion has allowed a new attitude toward the future to emerge. With the
new attitude forecasting became an essential activity.

Forecasting as an Essential Activity

The increase in the rate of change and in man's activity are the two
factors that make forecasting necessary.

The Acceleration of Change

Change is accelerating and its effects are so pervasive that it could be
said that the greatest single change would be the end of change itself. The
effect of change is cumulative because "the solution of each problem poses
new ones and reveals questions one had not imagined before solving the
earlier ones" (L'Allemand (6) p.237). In consequence, the more problems
solved, the more there are to solve. The right answer is one that asks the
right questions; for the same reasons, change creates further change.

Without change, tomorrow would be like today, but as the pace of world
development accelerates, forecasting its direction becomes more and more
essential. In fact, not to think about the future is, in a certain sense, a way
of dealing with it, but those who first become aware of future trends are best
placed to benefit from them. It is necessary to look ahead in order to make
the best use of opportunities.

Two different responses can be made to the increasing rate of change, the first, adaptive and passive; the second, active and deliberate. In the adaptive response, man seeks to make the best of change imposed on him, to "forecast the future in order the better to adapt to it," as Pierre Massé pointed out. It was as the result of this emerging need that forecasting grew into an autonomous discipline. But it was still piecemeal forecasting, as illustrated in the tendency to concentrate on predictions of technological change. The development of science and technology, once considered the "be-all and end-all," ignored the fact that science is only one product of society; the whole cannot be explained by the parts. In the more activist view, man acknowledges that his awareness of change may accelerate and direct change, and that as a consequence change is not just imposed. The part played by human action, however, remains marginal, since forecasting tends to seek a unique and predetermined future through an extension of the past. The uncertainty attaching to forecasting results does not stem from the fact that several futures are possible, but from the degree of precision with which the unique future has been described. This gives rise to the inherent contradiction, remarked by many authors, between action (which presupposes freedom of will) and forecasting (which assumes a certain determinism). While human action may be the cause of change, it is also largely conditioned by it, and, in this sense, human action makes forecasting necessary.

Action and Forecasting

"Prediction is made for action; one must know to be able to predict and predict to be able to dispose" (7, p.230). The faster change occurs, the less delay there must be between understanding it and making the necessary modifications to directions already taken. As Gaston Berger remarks, "The faster a car moves, the farther the headlights must reach." Decisions to be taken and actions to be launched require forecasting, first, because the results of our actions will occur in a world profoundly different from that in which they were taken, and second, because the long term usually determines the short term   (See Note 1); the desired end result determines the action. It should be noted, however, that while action makes forecasting necessary, forecasting is not neutral but determines action. "A simple change of forecast may, in producing its effects, lead to oscillations in a cyclical movement" (25). Thus, a plan, which can be defined as a few chosen objectives to be reached by a consistent set of means, has reality only by virtue of its objectives and therefore cannot exist without forecasting. Planning requires forecasting, but the making of forecasts leads, to a certain extent, to further planning and (in demography, for example) to the taking of corrective action.

Forecasting as a Flawed Activity

The inadequacy of forecasting techniques can be measured in terms of their repeated and substantial errors, as, for example, the inability to predict economic crises. The errors often make forecasting more misleading than useful and, to a large extent, explain what can be termed "the crisis in forecasting." The various causes of these errors merit a detailed analysis, which will be carried out later. It can be noted, however, that data cited from the past and present have significance only in the context of the theory in which they are considered. There are as many interpretations as there are theories.

Unfortunately, forecasting methods usually use only a single set of hypotheses and a single model. Furthermore, not only are the initial data incomplete but, after the model has been constructed, the hypotheses are forgotten. The more statistical the forecasts, the greater conviction they carry. Thus models built on quantitative data from the past, incomplete and liberally sprinkled with errors, usually are incapable of predicting a future that is not simply an extension of the past and which is qualitatively different from the present. Confusion often arises between forecasting and planning, a symptom that the term "forecasting" retains "the flavor of its strong and classical sense" of prophecy (24, p.24), seeking to reveal a future that is predetermined and unique, like the past. In the French National Plan, for example, forecasts become objectives; in the absence of a coherent view of the future of society, what is expected to happen is transformed into what is held up as desirable. On the other hand, in the Algerian Plan, objectives are frequently presented as forecasts. It would be preferable, in both cases, to distinguish what is desirable from what one thinks will happen, not to confuse forecast with objective - not to state, as in the French plan, that an unfulfilled objective was only a forecast; and not to blame, as in the Algerian plan, a forecasting error for an objective that was not achieved. Objectives result from choices and stand unchanged until they are revised, while forecasting is necessarily uncertain and must envisage a multiplicity of outcomes.

There is no single direction in the unfolding of history. Just as a given situation can result from several alternative lines of past development, so it, in turn, can give birth to several alternative future actions. However, we cannot merely take note of the inadequacy of forecasting; we must also explain it. Paradoxically, it is action that not only creates the need for forecasting, but which also causes many of its inadequacies.

R. Boudoin has written, "The fact that man is capable of desire, anticipation, and calculation is incompatible with an explanation in terms of causality" (8, p.26). Is this not what Keynes meant when he wrote, "Speculation often gets the better of enterprise"? He defined speculation as activity consisting of forecasting the psychology of the market, and enterprise as activity consisting of forecasting the estimated yield of capital throughout its existence (25). Thus "uncertainty is linked to human actions" (4, p. 56), and the pluralistic nature of the future is explained by the degrees of freedom of human action. It is man who forges his future. The recognition of this phenomenon is at the root of the prospective approach.

PROSPECTIVE METHODS, A CREATION OF THE FUTURE

The prospective approach grows out of awareness of a future that partakes of both determinism and of free will. It reflects a creative attitude toward a future that can be simultaneously experienced and shaped. "Prospective," first used by G. Berger in this sense, has become widespread in expressing this new attitude to the future. The word "forecasting" remains too strongly charged with its classic meaning of prediction and is used mainly in the sense of quantified calculations. Morgenstern was right to caution, however, that "all economic decisions have the characteristic that an infinite number of quantitative and nonquantitiative variables, have to be combined in a single act of decision" (33, p. 3).

To relate to the future, one must first relate to the past; what we regret about the past is usually the future ahead of it. Thus the past is merely a dead future, an extinct plan, and data are simply crystallized actions. The only determinism we grant the past consists of varying degrees of freedom that past actions have left us to act in the present so as to realize our future plans. What happens in the future results from our past actions, and what we desire explains our present actions. There is no exercise of will without an objective, and the objective of the will is to see our desires fulfilled. The plan based on wish leads to action; the past is always completed and the present is incessantly passing; only the future counts. "The future is the raison d'etre of the present," according to Grimaldi (p.8). The plan is produced by real or hypothetical gaps between what we have or expect to have or what we want to have. It is because there is a permanent transformation of "needs we want to fill into needs we are obliged to fill" (12) that "needs are unlimited and expandable" (31).

Thus, along with Henri Lefebvre we revalidate "wish fulfillment as a productive force" (27). May it not have been this that the young Marx meant when he referred to "material and spiritual productive forces" (31) and C. Fourier, to "production désirante"? To recognize wish fulfillment as a factor in producing the future leads us to revalidate subjectivity and utopianism and to reconcile poetic imagination with scientific reason; it provides insight into why a given structure of social relations collapses when the magnitude of the restraints opposed to wish fulfillment become intolerable.

"Utopia" is often wrongly taken as meaning the impossible. In fact, utopos means without place, i.e., that which does not exist, but which does not exclude the possibility of a future existence. We disagree that "Utopia is the road taken when action is deprived of meaning" (4). To the contrary, Utopia, insofar as it represents the essential fulfillment of a wish, is the source from which action draws its sense. The object of the prospective approach is to bridge the gap between the possible and the actual, to combat "the absurd," i.e., that divorce between the mind that desires and the world that disappoints (11).

The ultimate purpose of the prospective study is the launching of an action which, based on goals we see as fulfilling our wishes, will lead to a desirable future. Hence it is necessarily subjective in nature, since the future takes as many desirable forms as there are value systems. A fact is unique, but it lends itself to many interpretations.

The prospective approach is even more essential than forecasting because human action, which makes forecasting so inadequate, finds meaning in the prospective approach and also gives it meaning.

It should be emphasized that there is no single future resulting from an extension of the past, but rather a plurality of potential futures that one will be able to trace back from the future to the present, but that one cannot project ahead.

Therefore projection is not limited to forward-looking exploration but includes most particularly a "retro-vision," which consists of reexamining the paths that lead to the one (theoretical) future one has chosen, so that one may distinguish more clearly those paths that differ from them.

Forecasting constructs a future in the image of the past, but the prospective approach turns up a future radically different from the past, because problems change before they can be resolved, and anticipating these changes is more important than finding solutions to problems that time will have overcome. Human action accelerates and shapes change, but man is also shaped by this change, for example by past actions with which his future is intertwined. "Increased speed leads to greater time pressure and a greater feeling of harassment" (23, p. 365). But man does not so much bear the weight of the past as of the flood of current developments that push him around and mortgage his future. Thus "we have a tendency to overcommit the future, so when the future becomes the present we always seem to be in dire need" (23, p. 365).

There is certainly a contradiction in committing the future at a time when the future is becoming increasingly changeable and uncertain. (The contracting of long-term debt to cover purchase of a house illustrates this phenomenon.)

We should inquire as to the significance of this perpetual flight forwards, in so much as 'when I have no burdens I am bored, only emptiness is burdensome.' (L'homme encombré PUF, Collections prospective No. 15.) The prospective approach should guide our actions in such a way that our future is not in some way irreversibly damaged.

The prospective approach must contribute to retaining the greatest amount of fredom since what we do not like in the present is the result of possibilities that have been foreclosed through past action, while the attainment of those goals that meet our desires comes about through past actions that served to give us the freedom to move in many directions.

The prospective approach, which is the result of a new attitude toward the future, also requires a new attitude toward knowledge.

The juxtaposition utopia/science or reason/dream or madness disappears when we accept the possibility of a "revolutionary truth guided by our wishes (L'utopie retrouvée, Le Monde, June 2, 1972). We therefore agree with Andre Breton (9) when he writes, "I consider it completely inadequate to advocate the use of a single lever to the exclusion of all others."

"The absolute rationalism which remains fashionable only allows us to consider those facts which are closely connected with our experience; needless to say, experience itself sets its own limits; it is imprisoned in a cage from which it is increasingly difficult to get out. In the name of civilization, under the pretext of progress, we have managed to proscribe any kind of seeking after the truth not honored by custom." (9)

He who follows a single direction in his search cripples his thought. This can occur in two ways: from a lack of reasoning (to favor the emotional and inuitive at the expense of reason would be just as absurd as the contrary) or from the converse, here decried, which is perhaps what Fourier referred to as the "straying of reason," i.e., reason having gone astray and therefore in need of being righted, or to being itself an aberration that should give way to the attraction of the passions (the heart has reasons that reason knows not).

This crippled thought is characterized by its inability to create and imagine the future. Creation escapes it in the way the horizon always recedes as one approaches it. For such crippled thought, we propose to substitute total thought. Faced with this crippled man, product and progenitor of a mutilating and repressive society, where man is his own persecutor, we propose a liberated man for whom no path is necessarily closed and for whom wish is the main force determining the future.

Our horizon will not be fixed. This man, master of himself, will first be master of his own development and of the productive forces. He will no longer be torn apart by contradictions but will find in them the opportunity for continuous reassessment in which to redefine, liberate, and recreate himself. There will no longer be a divorce between man and his life, between his desire and reality. He will have mastered his existence.

When yesterday's utopia is today's reality, still another utopia can take shape. Change will no longer imply maladjustment, but equilibrium for man, who will be at home in his environment. Man and society will no longer be separated but will be carried along by the same structuring process, united in a single dialectic. The goal of the prospective approach will have been achieved; today's utopia will be transformed into tomorrow's reality.

Starting with history without prediction (forecasting as a contingent activity), we arrived at attempts to forecast history (forecasting as an essential activity) but this seemed to us doomed to failure (forecasting as a flawed activity) as long as the ultimate cause of change, action by man, presupposes freedom of will and is therefore unpredictable.

Forecasting in the classic sense of the word is possible only when man, through his past actions, has overcommitted his future to such a degree that the outcome can take only one or two forms.

The prospective approach implies a creative attitude to the future, radically different from attitudes classically adopted in forecasting; it recognizes the role of will in influencing the future and reinstates subjectivism and utopianism. Thus by starting from a criticism of what, for convenience, will be referred to as classical forecasting, we will describe the prospective method as a new approach to global, qualitative, and multiple prediction in the context of an uncertain future. This is the task of the first part of this study.

Criticism is of value only if it is constructive. Consequently the second part is devoted to a new prospective approach, which is intended to replace the old methodological framework, undermined by forecasting errors.

Finally, it must not be forgotten that the carrying out of actual prospective studies is both the origin and the proving ground of our theory, and therefore some concrete examples of this approach are presented in the third part.

2 Criticism of Classical Forecasting

FORECASTING AND ITS ERRORS

The economic history of industrial society has been marked by repeated forecasting errors (29). What is serious is not so much the existence of errors, as the systematic ignoring of past errors when a forecast is made. The more resounding its failures the more triumphantly it conducts itself. Thus, error becomes so widespread that it could begin finally to appear as one of the main characteristics of the profession. Consistent and repeated errors as, for example, the failure to forecast economic crises, are largely responsible for what can be called "the crisis in forecasting."

"The great crash of 1929 was not foreseen either in its timing or in its magnitude. The predicted shortage of energy became an overabundance of energy" (P. Massé) (6, p.99). At that time the gasification of coal and the exploitation of shale were already being seriously envisaged.

The subsequent discovery of oil in the Middle East explains this error but does not justify it. It was caused by lack of imagination and thought about the future. "Instead of imagining the future from the vantage point of the present, as is usual, it would have been more appropriate to judge the present by placing oneself in the future" (J. de Bourbon Busset) (6, p. 246).

The mistakes made in 1943 by Princeton demographers may also be cited. They predicted that the population of France would be 39 million in 1951, 38.1 million in 1960, and 36.9 million in 1970. (24, p. 212). The enormity of the error highlights the ridiculous precision with which the forecasts were presented.

In 1972, before what came to be known as the energy crisis, forecasts of energy consumption reckoned on the continuance of a declining trend in relative oil prices until 1980-1985. The present economic crisis is evidence, if that is still necessary, that errors can render forecasts misleading rather than useful.

Quantitative forecasting asks the questions and then participates in

10

formulating the answers. The basic mistake consists of considering these answers as the solution to the problem under consideration, particularly since an error in reasoning may easily be concealed in a correct forecast. "Even fallacious theories can lead to correct forecasts: an example is the Ptolemaic theory which allows the correct date of the next lunar eclipse to be calculated even though we are perfectly aware that the theory on which the calculation is based is wrong. A correct forecast does not prove the correctness of those which preceded it, nor the accuracy of the interpretations made from them" (Morgenstern) (34).

There are many causes of forecasting errors. It is possible, without claiming to be exhaustive, to group them into two large categories:

- Errors that apply to all forecasting, which result from the increasing difficulty of forecasting and which help to explain the difficulty of forecasting;
- Errors that are specific to classical forecasting, which result from its characteristics.

THE CAUSES OF ERRORS APPLYING TO ALL FORECASTING

The flaws in forecasting future events can be measured by the increasing number of errors committed in this field. Nevertheless some of these errors are difficult to avoid, and this is due to the nature of their causes; they certainly stem partly from the acceleration of change, but the root cause seems to be related to man, partly in his reactions to the very predictions made and partly through his use of knowledge.

Under this heading we may list the following:

- the announcement effect
- the inaccuracy of data
- arbitrary simplifications
- errors in interpretation
- epistemological obstacles

The Acceleration of Change

The acceleration of change causes both the necessity for and the inadequacy of forecasting. It in fact finds expression in the "irruption of the structural into the conjunctural." In so doing it causes the concept of "term" to lose the privileged role it still enjoyed ten years ago.

Short- and medium-term forecasting models including conjunctural and trend variables lead one to forecast developments which increasingly depend on structural variables. The concept of "term" and the variables associated with it do not stand up to change. If C. Goux (19) is correct in saying that the long term is the point at which the action of the structural variables becomes dominant, then greater emphasis should be laid on the long term, at the expense of the medium term. Thus the acceleration of change is reflected in a shortening of the medium term, leading eventually to its demise, as evidenced by the growing tendency to treat the study of what will happen in two to three years as long term forecasting.

The Announcement Effect

Publicity about developments one expects may in itself provoke reactions that in turn influence these developments. Under this heading fall self-fulfilling prophecies, i.e., those that come about through "ricochet effect" (for example, forecasting a high rate of inflation contributes to psychological fueling of such inflation) and, on the other hand, the "self-destroying" forecasts, i.e., those that do not come about because of the reactions (boomerang effect) the predictions set off. This latter type of error is sometimes desirable, and therefore sought after. In fact, "Forecasting a disaster is conditional; it is forecasting what would happen if we did nothing to stop it" (P. Massé) (6, p. 108). Demographic forecasting is an example of error actually sought after, in the sense that the warnings they afford us lead to action to correct the trend.

Usually, however, collective reactions to forecasts are uncontrolled. During the Korean war a lasting shortage of steel was forecast. This prospect led to such an upswing in activity that two years later the dearth had been replaced by a glut. Successive bouts of optimism and pessimism, i.e., behavioral cycles, explain economic cycles, and not the reverse. Other causes of forecasting error are associated with man's misuse of knowledge, i.e., inaccurate data, errors in interpretation, arbitrary simplifications, and epistemological obstacles.

Inaccuracy of Data

Inaccuracy will be defined by the three factors: error, uncertainty, and lack of precision (C. Ponsard) (35).

Not only are the available data insufficiently precise, they are also incomplete and strewn with errors. Morgenstern (33) asserts that the national income and consumers' purchasing power can probably not be known within an error of 10-15%. We agree with this author when he claims that "statistics are only an elaborate form of lies" and regrets that statistical data are published with no indication of the error in observation or estimation that may be involved.

Finally, considerable uncertainty surrounds the reliability of existing statistics and the results drawn from them. Morgenstern continues, "If one makes the simple observation that all rates of change are necessarily affected by errors, even if the errors are very small, e.g. two or three per cent of the quantities for which the rates of change are calculated, these rates become spectacularly different - frequently even with changes of symbol - from those calculated on the assumption of no observational error (D. Morgenstern) (33, p. 62).

Without knowledge of the errors, the input of economic data into high-speed computers is "an operation devoid of meaning." The same author mentions the following example of two almost identical systems, with radically different solutions:

Example 1 $\begin{cases} x - y = 1 \\ x - 1.00001y = 0 \end{cases}$ Example 2 $\begin{cases} x - y = 1 \\ x - 0.9999y = 0 \end{cases}$

Example 1 gives x = 100,001 and y = 100,000

Example 2 gives x = -99,999 and y = - 100,000

Furthermore available data are both incomplete and overabundant, the systems of equations often being simultaneously indeterminate and overdetermined, i.e., there are more equations than unknowns and more unknowns than independent equations. Korganoff and Parvu (24) describe the problem: "It even seems that these last two cases must actually be the law in a world where it is rare to obtain information in the appropriate quantity. There is usually either too much or too little."

Another example is of interest: Regular square matrices form an exception in the class of matrices, and in general even when matrices are square, they rank below the maximum and are singular. The solution of such systems therefore requires that extra conditions be imposed so as to give suitable approximations and smoothness. Considerable uncertainty attaches to the consequences of those conditions and therefore to the validity of the results. Such a situation arises when arbitrary simplifications are introduced, and this is another source of errors in forecasting.

Arbitrary Simplifications

As we have already emphasized, the information we possess is both incomplete and overabundant, the systems of equations are both indeterminate and overdetermined, and the corresponding matrices of these systems are singular. To say, for example, that a matrix is singular is to imply that it does not possess an inverse. In consequence, the corresponding system of equations has not a unique solution but rather an infinity of solutions among which a special solution is provided by the "pseudo-inverse" (26).

Mathematicians are strongly tempted to simplify the matrix arbitrarily, in order to make in invertible, and in this way to substitute a simple and unique solution for an absence of any solution or the presence of an infinity of solutions. Nevertheless, as shown in an example available at SEMA,* results obtained from an arbitrary simplification have sometimes no meaning even if the calculations are correct. The model has substituted itself for reality by

* SEMA - PROSPECTIVE, Groupe Metra, European consulting firm with headquarters in Paris.

distorting it, and in so doing has falsified the results. Error in the forecast is inevitable. In the example presented, the forecasting error is less discernible for the fact that a variation of $\pm 5\%$ in the modified coefficient does not change the final result. Apparently the sensitivity of the results to the arbitrarily introduced simplification is zero. This gives the results a spurious credit and reliability they do not deserve. In fact the result obtained after simplification does not correspond to a single one of the infinity of possible solutions applying when no such simplification is made. While the simplification is apparently minor, in terms of the consequences of the results, it is major.

Errors in Interpretation

Forecasting generally proceeds from assigning single meanings to data, when of course the single fact can have many meanings. The error in interpretation that results from this practice is at the heart of a great many forecasting errors.

As B. deJouvenel emphasizes, it is "because Marx regards history as a class struggle that the 1848 revolution is in his view nothing but a parody of the first French revolution... but others see in this revolution a dawning consciousness of nationalism which is going to spread throughout Europe" (24, p. 313). There is no independent reality of perception. The perception of facts depends on the theory we bring to them. Objective facts are nothing; they only exist through our subjective perception. "Data can only become scientific information through the agency of theory" (Morgenstern) (33).

Errors in interpretation are all the more difficult to detect since a false theory can yield correct forecasts. Conversely, a correct theory may be proved only much later or perhaps never, as testified by Einstein's theory of relativity.

Errors in interpretation are acceptable to the extent they represent gambles that the meaning one has assigned to data is the right one and that it will eventually be verified. To gamble is necessary because there are no absolute truths, only relative truths. Every proposition is true and so is its contrary and the only thing that counts is to know in what proportion it is true and in what proportion it is false.

As Pavel Apostol (2) (See Note 1) points out, even a single dialectic thesis-antithesis can lead to several different syntheses, each as valid as the others. This does not of course mean that they are equally probable. The human mind, however, does not readily concede this plurality, because to admit that several interpretations are possible is to make them all relative and therefore to diminish the importance of each. It may be difficult to see the forest for the trees. Finding one solution often leads to giving up the search for other solutions, and even to rejecting them when they are found. This attitude is explained in the "epistemological obstacles" theory developed by G. Bachelard (3).

Epistemological Obstacles

Certain forecasting errors are explained by our tendency to look at the "better lit" aspects of problems. The light dazzles us and hides from us what is beyond it.

We agree with G. Bachelard that "it is in terms of obstacles that the problem of scientific knowledge must be stated. In general, obstacles to scientific inquiry always present themselves in pairs, to the point where one might speak of a psychological law of the bipolarity of errors; as soon as one insurmountable difficulty appears, one can be sure that by turning the problem around one will run up against an opposing obstacle" (3). In the realm of science man had to overcome the obstacle of subjectivism, but in getting around that he ran into the obstacle of objectivism. Rational knowledge (science) stifles sentient knowledge (poetry). This is the "dialectical regularity of errors."

The permanent dialogue between theory and practice, which is the foundation of the principle of knowledge, is necessarily both subjective and objective since the scientist is himself part of the society he proposes to study. This dialogue must not be based merely on the intellectual but also on the emotional element. This represents the reinstatement of subjectivism (See Note 2), and of desire as influencing the future (See Chapter 1).

Finally, errors, and therefore the inadequacy of forecasting, can be explained not only, as was emphasized earlier, by the attitude toward knowledge, but by what C. Fourier called "the straying of his reason," as attested by the epistemological obstacles he refuses to surmount. Acceleration of change, inaccuracy of data, arbitrary simplifications, errors in interpretation, and epistemological obstacles are causes of forecasting errors that probably will never be completely eliminated. This does not of course permit us to relax our efforts in this direction. It appears, however, that another category of error, more specific to classical forecasting, could be rapidly removed.

CAUSES OF ERROR SPECIFIC TO CLASSICAL FORECASTING

Any approach to forecasting can be characterized in terms of several components:

- type of viewpoint adopted
- variables studied
- relationships envisaged
- explanation adopted
- future sought
- method employed

Usually, classical forecasting adopts a partial viewpoint, studies the quantitative variables, envisages static relationships, bases itself on the past as an explanatory key to a unique future, and seeks and uses deterministic models to carry out the forecasting. These specific characteristics of classical forecasting are responsible for numerous forecasting errors.

Partial Viewpoint

In the partial approach to forecasting, only some explanatory variables are adopted, and arguments of the type "all other things being equal" are used. Forecasts of energy consumption made in 1972 for the decade 1970/80 rested on the assumption of a continued drop in relative oil prices, without verifying whether this hypothesis would hold true even in case of changes in the world balance of power. The consequences of these forecasting errors are still being measured today.

Lack of foresight is related to Goldman's observation that "economic developments take on much of their character from the appearance within world society of an autonomous sector which acts more and more intensely and effectively on others, while becoming less and less subject to their influence" (17, p.22).

The economic discipline sets itself up as an autonomous sector. Economic forecasting is thereby cut off from social and political forecasting, and is itself parcelled up into technological, demographic, energy,... forecasting, in fact into many different branches that behave as though they did not belong to the same family.

Each discipline becomes autonomous and considers itself determining. This results in the juxtaposition of different isolated forecasts, each incompatible with the others. With the accelerating rate of change, however, everything is becoming more and more interdependent, everything acts on everything else, everything changes, "no other things are equal," and global forecasting becomes necessary.

Quantitative, Objective, and Known Variables

Since forecasters like figures, only quantitative variables are integrated into models. The models prove incapable of predicting changes produced by evolution in the qualitative variables, by "the irruption of the structural into the conjunctural." Moreover, as has already been emphasized, even if facts are objective, the perception of them and thus their interpretation are necessarily subjective. The variables used in forecasting, however, are usually considered as objective.

Advocates of forecasting refuse to question the objectivity of their variables and to build in nonquantitative variables because their models are not constructed for this. They attribute their errors to "the imperfection of the econometric models in relation to hidden variables" (Morgenstern) (33, p. 84). (Also see Note 3.)

It should be noted in passing that to name things is in a sense to suspend questioning about them. Shrouding these variables in mystery and describing them as "hidden" leads, whether they exist or not, to the end of any further search for them, to the inclusion only of known variables, and to accepting the validity of the forecasting model without further questioning.

Static Relationships

Classical methods of forecasting (trend extrapolation, mathematical and econometric models) assume the existence of stable relationships between the variables included, and behave as if the structures remained constant. This would be completely satisfactory in a slowly evolving universe, but it proves illusory in a world of rapid change.

Let us look at the classic correlation between energy and GNP: The level of energy consumption per inhabitant in the year 2000 is deduced from the GNP forecast for this same year, taking into account the correlation coefficient that applied in the past between these two variables. Notice that the variable considered "explanatory" (the GNP) is itself the object of a forecast that in turn may result from another forecast, but eventually it becomes apparent that time is being adopted as the "explanatory" variable. Certainly "it is sometimes easier to forecast the future consumption of a product from its past consumption than to find the explanatory variable," (C. Goux) (19, p. 201) but time is merely a pseudo-explanatory variable. Many forecasting errors result from confusion between collinearity and causality. Time explains nothing by itself. Variables explain only through their relationships to other variables, which are themselves in motion. Relationships are not static, but dynamic.

The Past Explains the Future

Numerous forecasting errors result when the future is explained in terms of the past. Econometric models, for example, forecast the future based on series observed in the past, and even if the variables change, they do so within static relationships. Thus in classical forecasting, not only is the future explained by the past, but it is also recreated in the image of the past. Each day brings further proof that this hypothesis is without foundation. In view of the acceleration of change, the future resembles the past less and less. As Paul Valery said: "The future is like everything else; it is no longer what is used to be."

In consequence, determinism, "the possibility of correctly predicting phenomena from data extracted from past or present observations," (10) is no longer possible.

We may ask whether this apparent inscrutability covers a hidden determinism, allowing us to understand what de Maria calls "entelechian" phenomena, or "the advent of new facts, whose a priori determination is completely impossible" (37). If these "entelechian" facts cannot be explained by what has gone on before, perhaps it is because the explanation is to be found not in the past, but in the future. C. Goux sees "the future as the key to the present" in the same way that G. Berger observes that "the present explains history and not the converse."

We do not reject the principle of causality, according to which there is no effect without a cause. But we feel that effects can be produced before causes and even where the cause never sees the light of day, for it is enough for man to anticipate an event or to believe that it will happen, to make him act as if it had already happened. The cause is psychological.

M. Friedman's theory of continuous income perfectly illustrates this explanation of the present by the future. According to this theory, an individual's consumption at any given time depends not only on his previous income but also on the future income he expects (16).

A Unique and Certain Future

Today's future will be tomorrow's past. The human mind proceeds by analogy. In noticing that the past is unique and that past facts are certain, it deduces that there will be only a single future and that the components of this future will gradually be unveiled and become certain.

A forecasting error frequently committed consists of getting carried away by this analogy and of concluding that, since but a single future will occur, this future is inevitable and no others are possible. This leads back to the concept of prediction as prophecy, whose object is to reveal a predetermined and therefore unique future.

In the minds of practitioners the uncertainty affecting the results of classical forecasting does not result from the fact that several futures are possible, but relates only to the greater or lesser precision with which this unique future has been projected. This is to be found in econometric models, in which the hypothesis of the normal distribution of the residuals leads to the forecast for C_t (consumption in the year t - explained by previous income) of a range of estimates within which, for example, it is 80-90% likely that C_t will occur. This notion of a single and certain line into the future (uncertainty affecting only the error in estimation) is the source of a great number of errors, because the future is multiple and uncertain.

It must be admitted that to forecast several forms of the future is difficult, because the validity of the reasoning leading to each form becomes relative. Unfortunately the potential number of forecasting errors is equal to the sum of probabilities that have been ignored.

Deterministic and Quantitative Models

A model is a simplified scheme of reality. Models used in classical forecasting (mathematical and econometric) are quantitative and deterministic. Any model can be considered a "black box," with input of data and output of results. A model is quantitative when the input data are quantitative variables and the result sought is a numerical forecast.

Errors arise when one accepts results as certain, while ignoring that, one, the input data are incomplete and contain errors, and, two, the choice of model is not neutral, but conditions the result. The black box embodies a theory, a reading of data whose value is limited by the fact that while there is a single set of data, they can lead to a multiplicity of interpretations.

Forecasting models are deterministic, i.e., "they prescribe successive stages of the system under consideration after the baseline data and the rules governing progressive changes have been stipulated (Boudon) (8). In classical forecasting, the past explains the future according to fixed laws, as in the exact sciences. But Berger (6, p. 18) states that "scientific law ignores history and only infers from the past to the future; it is really non-temporal."

To speak of economic laws is to forget that time is strongly charged with a sense of history, and so the same causes never produce the same effects and a given effect never has the same causes. Time sequences that have preceded the coming of an event do not necessarily, in economics, precede an identical event if they occur again. "Economic developments of today are never entirely determined by the events and conditions which immediately preceded them" (H. Bartoli) (5, p. 77).

Models are deterministic, but the past, present, and future depend largely on human actions based on the exercise of free will, which makes them uncertain. Furthermore, classical forecasting models are not only deterministic, but also quantitative, which is another source of forecasting errors, since the causes of change are not all quantifiable.

Quantitative models tend to reassure. Mathematics has become more and more sophisticated, and in watching its well-oiled mechanics at work, it is easy to forget that the hypothesis and choice of model determine the results achieved. "The use of mathematics does not in itself solve the problem, even if it allows the problem to be posed more rigorously... A system of false concepts remains a system of false concepts even when a whole body of theorems is rigorously deduced... The formulation of equations does not in itself confer scientific quality" (Amin) (1).

By simplifying reality for the pleasure of using mathematics, models have actually been transformed into schemes that distort reality. It is worth contemplating a sentence from Paul Valery: "Everything which is simple is false; everything which is complex is unusable."

Conclusion

Partial viewpoints, quantitative variables, the perception of relationships as static, the explanation of the future by the past, the search for a unique and predetermined future with the help of deterministic models, are all causes of error specific to classical forecasting. These errors derive from a passive or adaptive attitude to the future, in which action and freedom, the things that cannot be expressed by equations, have no place.

In order that the prospective approach may participate in the creation of the future by man and to avoid the errors that can occur, it must be provided with characteristics radically different from those of classical forecasting. Numerous forecasting errors and, in fact, the crisis in forecasting as a whole can be avoided by using the prospective approach - an approach with characteristics better adapted to the nature of the problems to be solved. It is in this sense that the crisis in forecasting has contributed to the emergence of the prospective approach.

3 The Prospective Approach To Systems: A Comprehensive, Qualitative, and Multiple Forecasting System

THE CHARACTERISTICS OF THE PROPECTIVE APPROACH

In order that the prospective approach can play a part in the creation of the future by man, it must be provided with characteristics radically different from those of classical forecasting. We are not trying to define the prospective approach here, but merely to identify some of its characteristics as seen from the forecasting viewpoint.

This is why the prospective approach adopts a comprehensive viewpoint, studies the qualitative variables whether quantifiable or not, incorporates dynamic relationships, adopts a multiple future as being the explanatory key to the present, and uses intentional analysis (structural analysis, cross-impacts, scenarios) as the forecasting method. It is because the future is multiple that it is uncertain (whether expressible in terms of probabilities or not), that it explains the present, and that its study introduces the need for international analysis. Thus, against classical forecasting, with its partial, quantitative and single approach, we set the prospective approach, an overall, qualitative, and multiple forecasting system.

An Over-All View

What we need to study are more and more complex systems in which everything is more and more interdependent (See Note 1) and in which the whole, as distinct from the sum of the parts, is reflected in each part. Since the parts are interdependent, reasoning based on a whole chain of arguments of "everything else being equal" cannot explain the evolution of such totality where everything moves at once. Everything acts on everything else; "nothing is equal." An understanding of the whole is necessary. The prospective method therefore involves placing the subject studied into the social and economic setting to which it belongs. The social and economic system is grasped as a complex structure composed of many linked substructures, and the behavior of each component substructure is clarified by understanding the structure as a whole.

Qualitative Variables

- Qualitative, quantifiable or not.

We start with the simple idea that the nonmeasurable elements may be determinant. We must therefore attempt to take into account as far as possible the qualitative, as well as the quantifiable. What is lost in mathematical formulas is gained in a closer approximation to reality.

- Subjective

Confronted by the future, personal judgment is often the only element of information available for isolating the factors likely to influence the course of events. The variables we adopt are not objective facts but rather judgments on whether certain events will or will not occur and how they will influence each other. To a certain extent, all variables are subjective, since the forecaster himself belongs to the society he proposes to study.

- Known or hidden

Two types of problems can be distinguished: 1) those of a logical nature, which can be related to a caregory of our experience, and for which a classical rational approach, on the face of it, is better suited, and 2) the others, which escape all known logic. Solutions to the latter type of problem are perhaps rational but the method of arriving at them is not necessarily so. A. Gordon (21) proposes synectics to allow the imagination to rise above the limited field of our experience. This is a research approach that consists of trying to solve a problem with elements taken from outside the subject - of putting into it what is outside of it and vice versa. He argues that we should "make the unfamiliar familiar and the familiar unfamiliar."

In our view the merit of this synectic approach, which allows counter-intuitive results to be obtained, goes back to the surrealists. In fact A. Breton presented just this, back in 1933, when he wrote: "To compare two objects as different as possible, and to convey to each one of them, whatever it is, a vigorousness which it lacked when taken into isolation.... the stronger the initial apparent dissimilarity, the more it must be overcome and denied" (9).

This is the method we propose to discover variables which may be essential for the development of the system studied.

Dynamic Relationships

In a universe in which all the variables change more and more rapidly, it is difficult to see why their relationships should escape this movement and remain immutable. Relationships are not fixed, they change; they are not static, but dynamic. In the study of the behavior of energy consumption, for example, what is important is not to project each of the explanatory "variables" (GNP, behavior, etc.) for the time period considered, and to proceed by simple homothesis, but to determine the overall change in the variables and in their relationships, because all the variables are interdependent, and each is explained by the others.

A Multiple and Uncertain Future

The past and the present are irreversible, unique, and certain, but the knowledge we have of them is incomplete, and even if the facts of the past are certain, they are but a tiny part of the great number of phenomena that make up reality. In consequence history is only a bet on one of many possible interpretations, because the fact is unique and its interpretation is multiple. By the same token, the future has many forms and so has the past, but for very different reasons.

In this connection it is worth mentioning Barel's point of view: The idea that there is only a single past and several futures is in part an optical illusion. It results from the implicit convention that the past is considered as a reality and the future as a set of hypotheses. It consists, to observe a distinction made by Karel Kosik, in assimilating historical facts into the historical reality instead of admitting that facts are a coded from of reality. There are certainly several futures, but also several pasts. On the level of reality there is only a single past and a single future; the optical illusion consists therefore of envisaging the past from the point of view of reality and the future from the point of view of fact (4).

The weight of possible error about the past and the uncertainty engendered by it lead us to speak of several pasts (several numbers are compatible with what we know). On the other hand, in relation to the future, it is the real multiplicity that causes uncertainty, rather than the converse. The future is yet to be; several eventualities are possible. The future is multiple, and the uncertainty (whether or not it can be expressed in terms of probability) attached to it is twofold. First, the future, which will actually happen, remains unknown. Second, an error (a deviation from a truth) can be committed in the assessment of the different possible outcomes. Concern over such an error is the object of uncertainty as it was in the case of the past. The plurality of the future explains and is explained by the degrees of freedom of human action. Among the many futures possible, the effective realization of one or the other will depend on what man has or has not done. The human will provide the driving force and we again encounter wish as a productive force in relation to the future (see Chapter 1).

This nondeterministic view of the future, in which human action is primordial, does not contradict the principle of causality, according to which there is no effect without a cause, since a single cause does not always produce the same effect but contains the seeds of a whole range of possible effects. Human freedom is therefore expressed through actions aimed at bringing different potentialities to fruition, attaining different objectives. It is the plurality of the future that makes it uncertain and the object of forecasting a double one: to identify the possible futures and to estimate (when possible) their probabilities of realization (taking into account, when appropriate, the actions that may be taken to achieve a desired outcome).

"The Future Explains the Present"

The prospective approach is based on a method of viewing history. We reject the thesis that a present state can be explained only in terms of the past. More appropriate is to explore the past and to explain it by reference to the present. This present should therefore be seen as "a dynamic and concrete state of tension between forces directed towards the future and forces operating in the contrary direction which tend to prevent its development" (Goldman) (18, p. 25).

The future should be seen as linked with the present, in the same way as the present explains the past. This throws some light on Professor Goux's formula: "the future, key to the present" (20). We are well familiar with the forces of the past, but to explain the present, we must also ask ourselves about the future. We better understand today the events that occurred in 1960; to understand what is happening today, we have to place ourselves in 1985 or beyond. With regard to the essentially subjective nature of reflection about the future, it is primarily the idea we form of the future that explains the present. For example, in basing an individual's consumption at a given moment on expected future income (theory of continuous income), Milton Friedman places importance on psychological factors. To say that production in a given year depends on price in previous years explains nothing in itself. What is important for the entrepreneur is his idea of the price in future years, relative or not to that of past years. This determines his production. The image of the future thus imprints itself on the present.

Intentional Analysis

When human action is restored to its rightful place in creating the future one is forced to recognize the initiatory role of the intention (wish as a productive force) of the different actors involved in the phenomena studied. Taking account of these strategies requires that "intentional" analysis be considered as a key method in the prospective technique. Intentional analysis (coined by G. Berger) (6, p. 24) means all methods that deal with variables of opinion (judgments, speculations, subjective probabilities...), such as structural analysis, Delphi techniques, methods of cross-impacts, the method of scenarios, etc. Since there are no real statistics of the future, personal judgment is almost the only available information.

Finally, appeal must be made to new methods that do not enclose the human mind in rigid formats, but allow imagination to be given free reign and permit the most to be made of the information that can be gathered. The second part of this study is devoted to presenting a certain number of methods we have developed for obtaining an over-all, qualitative, and multiple view of the future.

Conclusion

As opposed to the partial, quantitative, and single approach of classical forecasting, we have introduced the idea of the prospective approach - an over-all, qualitative, and multiple approach. This last characteristic, it should be noted, incorporates others, to a certain extent, because the future is multiple, uncertain (whether or not it can be expressed as probabilities), explains the present, and its study entails intentional analysis.

The increasing interdependence of all developments gives rise to the need for an overall viewpoint that prevents us from using arguments of the type "all other things being equal" and leads us to consider complex sets of interrelated elements, i.e., systems. It is thus with reference to this over-all point of view that we shall speak of the prospective approach to systems.

THE PROSPECTIVE APPROACH TO SYSTEMS

To define the prospective approach, it is not sufficient to contrast its characteristics with those of forecasting; it is also necessary to specify its goals, its limits, and to review its relationships with other forms of forecasting.

The Object of the Prospective Approach

The prospective approach has a double objective; it comprises both an exploratory stage of "forecasting" and a normative stage of "postcasting." The forecasting stage consists of an approach at three levels:

1. Exploration of possible futures, i.e., everything the imagination allows us to envisage.

2. Delimitation of feasible futures, i.e., everything possible, taking account of the material, human, and time constraints. (We prefer the word "feasible" to "plausible" because of the analogy with linear programming.)

3. Selection of desirable futures, according to the criteria of those who conduct the analysis.

The forecasting phase must be completed by a normative "postcasting," to allow the paths that lead to one possible future or another to be identified. It should be noted that the desirable is not necessarily realizable, and vice versa.

Goals and Limits of the Prospective Approach

The purpose of the prospective method is to prepare the way for the future adopted as an objective (both desirable and feasible). The prospective approach should guide our present actions so as to expand the field of the feasible of tomorrow. It should, in particular, lead to the careful consideration of decisions that by virtue of their irreversible effects, could prejudice the future or deprive it of a certain freedom of movement. A prospective decision is less concerned with maximum short-term advantage than with keeping a number of choices open in the future.

The prospective approach does have a limitation. It involves choices among basic hypotheses, and the results reflect a system of explicit or implicit values that are valid only to the extent that the system itself is acceptable. It is just this limitation that can render the prospective approach antidemocratic, because the underlying value system can be hidden in a haze of techniques.

Furthermore, the prospective approach, because of its "ideological aspect" lends itself to efforts to mobilize (or demobilize) mass support (for example, to accept current difficulties in favor of future benefits). This is the theme of generational sacrifice. It can lead in extreme cases to real ideological distortion "as if speaking of the future actually constitutes the future" (4).

This ideological role is also recognized by Marx when he writes, "whoever constructs a program of future society is a reactionary." Two interpretations can be made of this sentence. The first interpretation finds an echo in Bakunin, who said, "Any speech about the future is criminal because it impedes destruction, purely and simply, and halts the course of the revolution." The second interpretation condemns the existence of a program by virtue of its rigid structure, which is likely to overcommit the future and to oppose any change not anticipated.

The prospective approach represents the most comprehensive tool for examining the future and, in particular, makes use of long-term forecasting, an exploration based on the extrapolation of trends, a view of the future as a homothetic image of the present, and of planning, the normative obverse of long-term forecasting.

The classical correlation between consumption and GNP is an example of this loop. The level of consumption per capita in the year 2000 is derived from the GNP forecast for the same year. The normative approach completes the circular argument. Starting from this result, a program of productive investment is determined that will permit the goal to be achieved.

Technological forecasting is the forecasting of the evolution of science and technology. Science is a pure product of society and cannot therefore adequately explain its own functioning. Technology assessment is a recent term used to describe the practice already well known to economists of evaluating the side effects (spin-offs, etc.) that occur when certain projects are carried out.

SYSTEMS

We will not attempt to go into the different theories of systems, particularly since this subject has already been the object of several studies in France, two of which are cited. (13, 36). Our purpose is basically to present a functional definition of systems, to enable the reader to understand their development.

Definition of System

The definitions of a system are numerous. For a general and minimal definition, however, a system is

- a set of elements (of parts, or variables)
- a set of relationships applied to these elements.

In fact, a system does not exist outside the perception one has of it. (See Note 2). The transformation of a set of interacting elements into a system must be considered a product of the will of the observer. "A system is not the outside world, but a way of looking at it" (Fortet) (36, p. 5).

Elements can be concrete or abstract entities or events. The definition of an element calls for a certain number of data that can be classified into two major categories: qualitative (in particular existence or not) and quantitative. The existence of <u>relationships</u> between the elements of a system is reflected in two types of effects: the modification of certain quantitative characteristics and the appearance or disappearance of qualitative characteristics. It should be noted that an element exists or is defined only by virtue of its relationships to other elements. Naturally there can be no quantitative data without qualitative data. One cannot assert that a variable has a particular measurement without first admitting the existence of this variable. The single definition of an element may not be the only one possible. There are as many possible definitions as there are different viewpoints.

Along with DeLattre (13) we distinguish between a functional definition (which contains all the qualitative and quantitative characteristics necessary to account with certain precision for the role and behavior of an element in one system studied) and an exhaustive definition (which would give an account of the role and behavior of the element in all possible systems).

Characteristics of a System

First of all, a system is in motion; a system is dynamic. Time plays an important part in the concept of a system. Next, a system is global; it comprises a whole, not reduced to the sum of its parts, in such a way that the development of the parts can be explained only by that of the whole. This global nature confers on the system an autonomy sufficient to assure its self-reproduction. Finally, a system is complex. Like Jantsch (49), we would describe as complex a system with multiple nonlinear feedback loops and retroactive effects.

The complexity manifests itself in the impossibility of describing the whole system and deducing its behavior from knowledge of its elements, since not only is the whole different from the sum of its elements, but also the behavior of each element depends on the behavior of the whole. The whole is thus contained in each part (it has an organic life), and, in consequence, reasoning based on a whole chain of "everything else being equal" assumptions is inappropriate for explaining the behavior of such a system in which everything moves at once. In a dynamic system, "nothing else is equal."

States and Structures of a System

By definition, a system is dynamic; its transformation over time is explained by the change in the relationships between its component elements and by the effects of these relationships on the elements themselves. The state of a system at a given moment is therefore the specification of:

1. The elements characterizing this system, accompanied by a standard of measure.
2. The nature of the relationships between these elements.

A system is in perpetual evolution. The structure of a system for a given period is the specification of:

1. The elements characterizing the system, without measured values.
2. The relationships existing between these elements, without specifying their nature or their importance.

Thus the structure of a system is a relational arrangement between the elements of the system without specifying the nature of these relationships. The latter can change (evolution of the state) while the arrangement remains the same. The structure of a system is much more permanent than the state. It represents the key to the evolution of the system for a whole time period.

Prospective Reading of Systems

The seven characterics of the prospective approach as distinct from those of classical forecasting (See Table 3-1) form the frame of reference for the prospective study of systems.   Three levels of understanding are distinguished: 1. apprehension, 2. comprehension, and 3. explanation.
1. Apprehension consists of delimiting the boundaries of the system that contains the subsystem being studied and, conversely, of breaking it down into its observable systems with an acceptable degree of complexity.
2. Comprehension consists of defining the structure, i.e., the variables that characterize the system, and the relationships between these variables.
3. Explanation consists of identifying the main driving forces and mechanisms of the system so that its dynamics of change can be specified.
There is an unequivocal link between 1 and 3.   Obviously, before understanding a problem, the elements that give rise to it must be apprehended.
The step from comprehension to explanation deserves more attention. It is useful here to refer to L. Goldman (17) p. 1009: "The comprehensive description of the genesis of an over-all structure has an explanatory function in the study of the behavior of particular structures which form part of it; comprehension and explanation in this context are but a single intellectual process related to two different reference groups: those of the wider system and those of the system within it."
Since an explanation of a given system is provided by understanding the structure of the wider system, we are constrained, in studying the prospective of a particular phenomenon, to consider the wider system in which it occurs.

CONCLUSIONS: CLASSICAL FORECASTING COMPARED WITH THE PROSPECTIVE METHOD

The repeated errors of forecasting and, in particular, the absence of forecasts of economic crises have given rise to the crisis in forecasting, which has contributed to the emergence of the prospective approach, i.e., the creation of the future by man, whose wish is the main force behind change. The prospective approach, an overall, qualitative,and multiple method of forecasting, can be distinguished from classical forecasting in terms of the seven characteristics presented in Table 3-1.
History is made by human action.   Actions already undertaken leave behind them a certain determinism, whereas possible future actions leave man free to choose from among the whole range of potential futures the one he wishes. His wish is thus the force that creates the future. The apparent contadiction between determinism and action that presupposes freedom is overcome by the systems approach.

TABLE 3.1 Characteristics of Classical Forecasting Compared with Those of
the Prospective Method

	CLASSICAL FORECASTING	PROSPECTIVE APPROACH
Viewpoint	Piecemeal "Everything else being equal"	Overall approach "Nothing else being equal"
Variables	Quantitative, objective, and known	Qualitative, not necessarily quantitative, subjective, known or hidden
Relationships	Static, fixed structures	Dynamic, evolving structures
Explanation	The past explains the future	The future explains the past
Future	Single and certain	Multiple and uncertain
Method	Deterministic and quantitative models (econometric, mathematical)	Intentional analysis Qualitative (structural analysis) and stochastic (cross-impacts) models
Attitude to the future	Passive or adaptive (future <u>comes</u> about)	Active and creative (future <u>brought</u> about)

II

The Scenarios Method

Introduction

To implement the prospective approach (defined in Part I), we must use new methods, radically different from those of classical forecasting, to free the human mind from the constraints of a rigid framework and give full scope to the imagination.

The great diversity of methods developed to meet this need and currently applied in the study of the future (futurology) does not prevent the construction of a typology, as certain authors have skilfully shown (38, 49, 56). The reader is referred specifically to these works. The purpose here is not to provide an inventory of methods but to offer guidelines linking together certain methods relevant to a prospective study which at least have the merit of being proven.

The methodology presented in this second part of our study does not represent a panacea, but merely one possible approach among others. These should not necessarily be excluded, but integrated where useful and necessary. It should be noted that while the approach described here applies to a great number of problems of the prospective approach, it should nevertheless be adapted to suit each particular case. It should be noted also that most of the methods that comprise this approach are not drawn from established practice, but are the fruit of teamwork carried out since 1972 in implementing prospective studies of air transport, energy, chemicals, international relations, etc.

Finally, it should be observed that the word "prospective" remains inseparable from the word "system" as, for example, is illustrated by the title "The Prospective and Systems Analysis," chosen by Barel (4) in publishing in 1971 the remarkable work he carried out for the Délégation en aménagement des territoires et action régionale (DATAR) of the Ministry of the Interior. The expression "systems analysis" has become widespread, particularly in the social sciences. The term does not refer to a particular method but to a spirit of working, an attitude of seeking. Unfortunately, this expression is often misused. Systems analysis has become a fashionable catchword used to describe even methods that are contrary to its spirit, as is illustrated by the International Institute for Applied Systems Analysis (IIASA) questionnaire. We shall therefore adopt the definition given by Barel: "Systems analysis, in the majority of cases, consists of bringing out the fact that the objective examined must be seen in a wider context than the original system, and the term analysis serves to emphasize that it is useful to break compex problems down into their component elements."

4 Structural Analysis, A Comprehensive and Qualitative Approach

A system presents itself in the form of a set of related elements. The relational fabric between the elements (the structures of the system) merits our attention because it holds the key to the dynamics of the system and because it displays a certain continuity. The purpose of structural analysis is to bring out the "structure" of relationships between the qualitative variables, whether quantifiable or not, that characterize the system. This exercise has the advantage of providing greater insight, while permitting the analysis to pass through the three levels of "understanding" defined above:

- Appprehension
- Comprehension
- Explanation

APPREHENSION OF THE SYSTEM

Apprehension consists of defining the boundaries of the system of which the phenomenon under study is a part, in the form of a subsystem. We establish a list of variables that characterize the subsystem and its environment. To identify as exhaustibly as possible the list of variables characterizing the system, no line of research is excluded a priori; all creative devices are valid (brainstorming, synectics, morphological analysis, etc.)

In general, case studies should be assembled, taken apart and reassembled, and discussed. In order to discover the variables, the matter should be examined from different political, economic, technological, psychological vantage points. When a new variable comes to mind, the question should be asked whether it bears even a remote link to the list already established; if it does, it is retained; otherwise, rejected. This effort continues until

35

imagination and sources of information are exhausted. As a final step, all the variables previously rejected are reconsidered in the light of the final list, and some of them may be reinstated. Furthermore, when we speak of a relationship, we speak entirely in qualitative terms, almost intuitively without bothering to determine whether the link is direct or indirect, positive or negative. Finally, the list of variables built up is never totally exhaustive, but remains limited by our imagination. This would, however, be even more the case if advantage were not taken of structural analysis.

COMPREHENSION

Comprehension consists partly of a final inventory of the variables characterizing the system, and partly of plotting their relationships in a structural analysis matrix.

Inventory of Variables

The enumeration of the variables begins with the list built up in the earlier exercise. Some additions and deletions are made, so that a relatively homogeneous list is obtained. It is often wise, depending of course on the nature of the phenomenon being studied, to carry out an a priori grouping of internal and external variables. Internal variables are those that characterize the subsystem under study, and external variables are those that comprise its environment. Simple though this idea may appear, a concern not to distort the inquiry by a priori structuring of the data has in the past prevented its use. Only recently, on the occasion of a prospective study of a country and its external environment, was this breakdown introduced. It has since been used almost systematically for all new prospective studies we have undertaken. Unfortunately, the concrete examples considered in the third part predated this development and do not therefore make use of this distinction.

Finally, a detailed explication of the variables is made because this is necessary for a complete understanding on the relationships under study. This process of definition allows everything included under the heading of the particular variable to be held in awareness. Without the creation of this agreed language, the consideration or determination of the relationships would be impossible or would make no sense. The records thus established remain open, are gradually completed, and represent a systematic sorting of information.

Identification of Relationships and Structural Analysis Matrix

In the structuralist view of the world, a variable exists only through its relationships.   Furthermore it is the intuitive perception of certain relationships that has allowed us to assess this or that variable during the setting up of the list of N variables that characterize the system.

The N variables, written in the rows and columns of a double-entry table, form what is called a structural analysis matrix, which is merely the matrix of the direct relationships between the variables. The matrix can be assembled in either of two ways, i.e., either linear, noting the influence of each variable on each of the others, or columnar, noting by which variables each variable is influenced. Theoretically, both procedures should be employed, and a comparison of the results obtained by superimposing the two matrices on each other will draw attention to the differences and therefore the errors that have arisen. It should be stressed, however, that often this practice proves to be a luxury the user can rarely afford. Most of the structural analysis hitherto carried out contained several dozens of variables - in general around 100 - and there are around ten thousand questions to be asked. This represents several weeks of unremitting labor.

Structural analysis represents a process of systematic inquiry. Without the help of this matrix, there would be, among the ten thousand questions, many that would never be asked. Furthermore, the completion of such a matrix must be carried out by at least two or three persons so that different points of view are brought to bear and nothing is left to chance. However, with more than four or five persons, the discussion becomes more difficult than fruitful.

In general, when dealing with about 100 variables, creating the matrix consists simply of identifying the direct relationship between variables without asking whether they are negative or positive. In fact, this is not always obvious, and furthermore it might call into question the choice of heading under which the variables are listed, since, contrary to what might be thought, changing a variable from plus to minus, or the other way around, does not necessarily result in a change in all linear or columnar relationships. An example is consumption as a function of income. When income increases, consumption increases. When income decreases, consumption does not necessarily decrease, because of the "ratchet effect." Nevertheless, in problems of more restricted size it is possible, and sometimes even fruitful, to distinguish positive and negative influences. This was done during a first experiment (62), and the information derived can be used in a particularly interesting way, i.e., in the demonstration of positive feedbacks (amplifiers) and negative feedbacks (regulators).

We draw on intuition to recognize relationships between system variables. While such intuition may sometimes allow a correlation between two given variables to be identified, it does not allow us to establish definitely the existence of a direct relationship. The intuitive apprehension of an influence of variable (a) on variable (b) can only lead to a decision in favor of the existence of such a relationship after having asked the following three questions:

1. Does variable (b) influence variable (a)?

The intuitive identification of a correlation between two variables (a) and (b) sometimes leads to a misapprehension of the direction of this influence. Conversely, recognizing an influence of (b) on (a) does not necessarily preclude an influence of (a) on (b).

2. Does variable (a) influence (b) through the intermediary of a third variable (c)?

The influence of variable (a) on variable (b) may very well work indirectly, the path from (a) to (b) passing via other variables. The possibility must therefore be considered of an influence of variable (a) on variable (b) through the intermediary of a third variable (c). The existence of an intermediary variable does not necessarily preclude a relationship of direct influence between the first two variables (a) and (b).

3. Are variables (a) and (b) both influenced by the same variable (c)?

Correlation does not imply causality. Two correlated variables (a) and (b) may have no causal link between them when they are both influenced by the same variable (c). Conversely, the direct influence of a variable (c) on the two variables (a) and (b) does not preclude a link between the latter. Finally, once these questions have been asked for each pair of variables in the system, the structural analysis matrix appears in Fig. 4.1, where

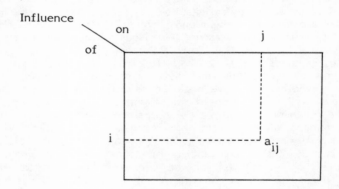

$$a_{i_j} = 1 \quad \text{if a change in variable i implies a change in variable j;}$$

$$a_{i_j} = 0 \quad \text{otherwise.}$$

EXPLANATION

The structural analysis matrix allows the structure of the system to be brought out and the explanation stage to be undertaken through a "reading of the matrix." This reading comprises the study of both direct and indirect effects or feedbacks.

The Study of Direct Effects

In counting the number of influences of each variable on each of the others, and the number of variables by which each variable is influenced, it is possible to distinguish those variables of a primarily "motor" nature from those of a primarily dependent nature. In fact a high linear total signifies a variable dominating the others, while a high columnar total reveals a dependent variable, very sensitive to the action of others. Since the matrix is not symmetrical, the two hierarchies are not reciprocal, and they can be represented in a single graph, as suggested by P.F. Teniere Buchot (56, p. 174). The study of direct effects does not, however, seem an adequate framework for explaining the system. In practice a variable may very well be neither dominant nor dependent, while nevertheless representing an essential element of the system structure, because of the importance of its indirect relationships. This is illustrated in Fig. 4.2.

The Study of Indirect Effects

To determine the most important variables, the idea that immediately comes to mind is to classify the variables according to the number of their direct relationships. Subsystems S_1 and S_2 would be independent if not linked by the intermediary of variables (a), (b), and (c).

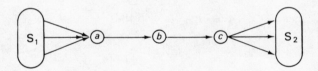

Fig. 4.2 Indirect Effects

In terms of direct effects, (a) is very dependent on subsystem S_1, and (c) dominates the subsystem S_2.

This analysis tends to neglect variable b, which nevertheless comprises an essential element in the system structure, because it is the relational link between the two subsystems S_1 and S_2.

We have shown, however, that this idea proves inadequate, because only the direct interactions are taken into account. It is necessary to consider both the direct and the indirect effects that a movement in one of the variables can have on the other variables, or on itself through reaction loops or feedbacks. A simple calculation shows that in a matrix of this type there are millions of such feedback effects. The human mind is incapable of simultaneously picturing and interpreting the huge variety of possible relationships. Fortunately computerized data processing can help in this task. This is the purpose of the MICMAC method. MICMAC, a French acronym signifying cross-impacts matrix multiplication applied to a classification, was developed in 1972-1974 in collaboration with J.C. Cupperin. It actually investigates the number of indirect relationships relating the variables with each other, i.e., the feedbacks and chains of influence.

The principle on which the method is based, repeated matrix multiplication, will be presented, together with two practical variants of the method, standard MICMAC, and MICMAC in blocks.

Powers of Matrix

Suppose we have a square Boolean matrix, with all its elements equal to 0 or 1. This matrix can be multiplied by itself using the conventional algebraic rules. Let A (n, n) be such a matrix, which is actually the structural analysis matrix.

Order 1. $A = a_{ij}^1$

with $a_{ij}^1 = 1$ if there is a positive or negative influence of variable i on variable j, in which case it will be said that there exists a chain of influence of length 1 linking i to j.

Order 2. $A^2 = A \times A = a_{ij}^2$

where $a_{ij}^2 = \sum_{k=1}^{n} a_{jk}^1 \cdot a_{kj}^1$

In particular, when $a_{ij}^2 = 1$, there is a k such that

$$a_{ij}^2 = a_{ik}^1 \cdot a_{kj}^1$$

In other words, we have an intermediate variable k such that the i variable has an impact on the k variable which in turn has an impact on the j variable:

$$i \text{———————— } k \text{ ———————— } j$$

We then say that there is a chain of influence of length 2 linking i to j. When $a_{ij}^2 = 2$, there exist k_1 and k_2 such that

$$a_{ij}^2 = a_{ik_1}^1 \cdot a_{k_1 j}^1 + a_{ik_2}^1 \cdot a_{k_2 j}^1$$

In other words, there are two such intermediate variables and we say that there are two chains of influence of length 2 linking i to j.

When $a_{ij}^2 = L$, there are L such variables $k_1, k_2, ..., K_L$, and we say that there are L chains of influence of length 2 linking i to j.

Order n. When $a_{ij}^n = L$, there are L chains of influence of length n linking i to j.

The special case of i = j

$a_{ij}^1 = 0$ Since a variable is assumed not to have an impact on itself, the first diagonal is zero.

$a_{ij}^2 = L$ There are L chains of influence linking i to i. Chains of this type are called circuits, and we say that i is involved in L feedback loops.

When $a_{ii}^n = L$, then the i variable is involved in L feedback loops of length n. The i variable is considered a node of L feedback loops of length n.

Standard MICMAC Method

When dealing with a complex system, the choice of variables cannot be disassociated from the choice of relationships. To repeat, a variable exists only by virtue of its relationships with others, and choosing the variables is thus inseparable from choosing the relationships. It should also be noted that the most interesting relationships are those that by producing feedback effects provide for the dynamics of the system.

It therefore seems reasonable to consider the feedback loops or circuits of influence passing through each variable, and to adopt as the first classification criterion, the number of feedback loops in which each variable is involved. This is the standard MICMAC method.

As was seen above, each time the matrix is raised to a further power, the number on the main diagonal tells us the number of feedback loops of which the corresponding variable is the node. In practice the foregoing results are not completely correct. In fact, during successive increases in the power of the matrix, the shorter feedback loops string together to form longer ones; certain elements are therefore counted several times in the same loop. In doing so, too much emphasis is laid on the variables involved in short feedback loops, which is not unreasonable, since the longer are less significant in terms of impact on the system (taking account of the latency period).

As the powers increase, i.e., with increasing length of feedback loops, the rankings obtained by MICMAC are compared. In practice this classification tends to stabilize rapidly. The order obtained for feedback loops of length p being stable, this is chosen as the final ranking.

The greater the density of relationship in the matrix, the more rapidly stability is achieved. In applying MICMAC to the POPOLE model, stability of classification is reached from the 7th power cf (57). Although the theoretical demonstration of this stability remains to be carried out, in practice this stability has occurred in the ten cases or so in which the method has been applied.

The hierarchy obtained

MICMAC produces a ranking of the variables, which can be compared with that obtained from considering the number of direct relationships between them. In particular, certain variables that, in terms of direct impact, might appear secondary emerge as being very important when the number of feedback loops in which each variable is involved is considered. Thus, for example, the application of MICMAC to the POPOLE model (57), shows that the variables in water policy have much greater influence on the system in terms of their indirect effects than would have been apparent merely from a consideration of the direct effects, which were so limited that some of these variables were discarded in subsequent stages of the analysis.

Another example deserves mention to illustrate the method. In many regards it is the origin of the methods presented here. This is the prospective study of nuclear energy undertaken at the Commissariat à l'énergie atomique (CEA) in 1972, and since pursued in collaboration with Electricité de France (EDF) (62-64).

The development of nuclear energy is a complex phenomenon, related not only to technical and economic variables (investments, yields, degree of energy independence, consumption of energy, electricity prices...), but also social (choice of the type of growth and of society, lifestyle...) and ecological (awareness of environmental problems, pollution, including thermal, aesthetic by waste matter, etc...). After taking into account political, economic, technological, and other factors, the study group set up to undertake the prospective study of the development of nuclear energy in France adopted a list of 51 variables suitable for consideration. See Fig. 4-3.

The variable "sensitivity to external effects" moves from the 5th to the 1st position. Thus, since 1972, structural analysis has allowed us to grasp the importance of collective psychology and of public opinion in the development of nuclear energy.

This variable explains the debate about nuclear energy that began a while ago in France, and among whose first effects is a slowing down of the program initially envisaged by Electricité de France (EDF). It is remarkable to notice that the same variable now named "awareness of the environment" instead of "increasing sensitivity to external effects" is ranked highest in the order established by the EDF team in relation to the same problem.

The variable "problems relating to sites for nuclear power stations" moves from 32nd in the first ranking to 10th in the second; the variable "accidental nuclear catastrophe," from 26th to 15th place. This means that the long-term indirect effects (particularly psychosociological) of an accidental nuclear catastrophe are, all things considered, greater and more lasting than the immediate effects (thousands of deaths, public reaction...).

This change in ranking reflects the well known "fear of the atom" so

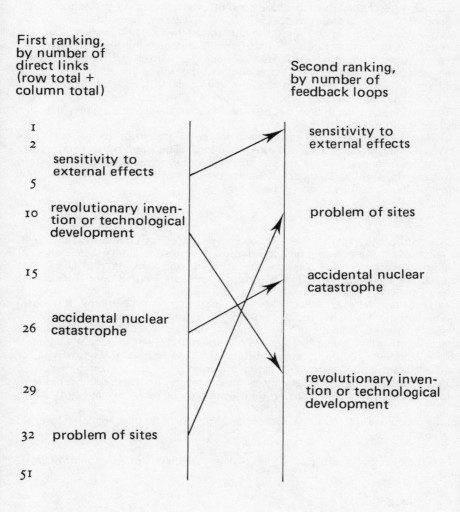

Fig. 4.3. Change in ranking of certain variables considered in a prospective study of the development of nuclear energy in France.

potent nowadays, which is largely explained by the atomic explosion of Hiroshima 30 years ago.

On the other hand, the variable "revolutionary invention or technological development" drops from 10th to 29th place in passing from the first to the second ranking. This shows that the inertia of the system is such that the repercussions of this variable are less important than would be thought from an examination of the direct effects. It should be pointed out that the results of the standard MICMAC method should not be taken too literally. They should simply serve as an aid to thought, particularly through bringing out a new hierarchy of variables which supports the intuitive belief in the importance of some variables, but also denies it through some results that are completely counterintuitive.

MICMAC therefore forces persons involved in the study to ask questions that would not otherwise have come to mind. This method is particularly useful when means are being sought to reduce the complexity of the system by limiting the field of study to variables considered essential from the point of view of the dynamics of the system.

MICMAC Block Method

A second application of the method, much more instructive than the first, is possible when the system considered allows the distinction between internal variables specific to the phenomenon studied, and external variables that comprise its environment. The structural analysis matrix then consists of blocks as shown in Fig. 4-4.

Raising the over-all matrix to successive powers remains the basic principle of the MICMAC block method. But this time we are particularly interested in what happens in each block. Consider block 3, for example. It gathers together the set of influences of the environment (external variables) on the subsystem studied (internal variables). The method gives two types of results of particular interest: first, a ranking of the external variables according to their impact on the internal subsystem, and, second, a ranking of the internal variables according to their sensitivity to the environment.

Ranking of External Variables According to Their Impact on the Internal Variables

External variables are ranked in two ways: direct ranking and MICMAC ranking.

Direct ranking

With each external variable is associated the number of direct relationships of this variable with the internal variables (identified by reading one row of block 3 external-internal of the structural analysis matrix.) A ranking is thus established of the external variables according to their potential direct impacts.

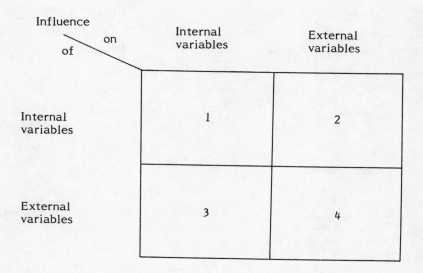

Fig. 4.4 Structural analysis matrix for MICMAC block method.

Block 1 shows relations between internal variables; 2, influence of internal variables on the environment; 3, influence of the environment on the internal subsystem; and 4, relations between the external variables.

MICMAC ranking

With each external variable is associated the number of indirect relationships or paths of the given length running from the variable being considered to all the internal variables (the sum of the appropriate row in the external-internal block of the whole matrix raised to the appropriate power). For each power of the matrix, the external variables are ranked in decreasing order according to the number of such paths. In general this ranking becomes and remains stable before the 10th power is reached.

We thus obtain a ranking of the external variables according to their impact on the internal variables (in terms of indirect effects). It is highly instructive to study the changes in the hierarchy between these two rankings, particularly when we are interested in the changes by groups of variables.

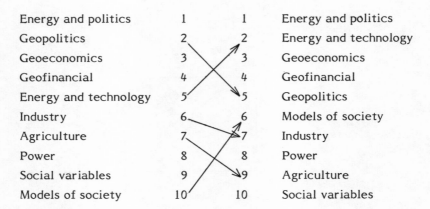

Fig. 4.5 The ranking of groups of variables changes as shown when we
successively examine direct relationships and then the indirect
influences on the internal variables.

This diagram is related to a prospective study carried out on behalf of a
foreign country, looking at its external relationships. The results cannot be
presented here because of the confidential character of the study.

Some groups of external variables prove to have a much greater impact
than would be thought from simply examining the direct influences. This is
the case for the groups "energy and technology" rising from 5th to 2nd place
and "models of society" rising from 10th to 6th place.

This interpretation of the results of MICMAC by groups of variables must
be complemented by a study of the hierarchy of variables inside each group.

Ranking of Internal Variables According to Their Sensitivity to External
Variables

As before, the internal variables are subjected to a direct ranking and a
MICMAC ranking. But this time the column totals of the external-internal
block of the over-all matrix are of interest. With each internal variable is
associated the number of direct relationships and indirect relationships
passing from the external variables to the internal variable under consideration. Interpretation then proceeds as before, and produces a hierarchy of
internal variables (grouped or not) according to their sensitivity to the
environment. Analogous to a roadmap of the frontier between two countries,
these two rankings identify the most important points of exit and entry. It is
useful to complement the interpretation by studying the potential traffic
between these crosspoints, in other words, to carry out an analysis of the
indirect relationships between the external and internal variables.

Analysis of the Indirect Relationships Between the Two Classes of Variables

Consider block 3 (external-internal) of the matrix produced. A simple computerized calculation immediately gives the number of indirect paths from all the external variables to all the internal variables. The intercomparison of frequencies provides an ordering of the indirect relationships between the two classes of variables, which in fact amounts to ranking pairs of variables.

In this way, we can show that one external variable or another has an important impact on the internal subsystem because of specific indirect relationships. Furthermore, the row and column frequencies provide some "quantitative" information about the hierarchy between groups of driving external variables and sensitive internal variables, by specifying the proportion of each group in the total number of indirect relationships in the "external-internal" block.

Thus, in the example mentioned above, the first two groups of external variables obtained by MICMAC, "energy and politics" and "energy and technology," account between them for almost 60% of the total of indirect effects of the environment on the internal subsystem studied.

Furthermore, the ordering of linear and column totals corresponding to the ranking of external and internal variables mentioned above takes the form of a decrease, which would be regular if there were not certain discontinuities, in particular between groups that undoubtedly display strongly related components (subsystems of variables).

It should be noted that the structural analysis matrix lends itself to other mathematical treatments, some of them very useful. Examples include the seeking of strongly connected components, i.e., of independent subsystems, and, when the sign of the direct relationship is known, the analysis of positive and negative feedbacks (the MICROBE program) (65). Mention should be made of the analysis of data (principal component analysis and factor analysis) which can sometimes be very powerful in seeking certain hidden explanatory factors (principal axes), and, finally, for identifying the structure of the system. However, these methods are described elsewhere (see Note 1).

Extensive research is being undertaken to gain the maximum benefit from the structural analysis matrix, but methods often resort to sophisticated techniques that have nothing to do with the reality being explored. Quantification is prone to lead to the underestimation of those factors that cannot satisfactorily be quantified. Relationships are not in fact always quantifiable, and even less is known about the time lags between two variables. Reality is blurred, and there is no point in trying to measure a mountain with a ruler.

Research in this field should nevertheless be taken seriously, and in certain cases such work is undoubtedly of interest (see Note 2).

CONCLUSION

The analysis above can be extended without difficulty to any block of the structural analysis matrix, but often the external-internal block is of greatest interest. Planning at corporate, sectoral, or national level usually makes use of an over-all analysis of the dependency relationships of the systems studied with their environment. Identification of the internal variables that are most sensitive to this environment and of the external variables that are most influential is a vital stage in the prospective study of the system considered. In fact, the sensitive variables and influential variables as defined above can rightly be considered the essential variables on which a prospective study should concentrate.   If the interest is in the over-all dynamic of the system, however, and if it is not decomposable into blocks, then the results of standard MICMAC will be adopted.

The results of MICMAC should not of course be taken too literally. One should never be the prisoner of a model, but rather draw lessons from it so as to be able to make a better final choice. In particular, the MICMAC ranking has nothing to do with the probabilities of occurrence of each variable, but means rather that if such a variable occurs then it will have important repercussions on the whole system. One may thus be led to reject such a variable in spite of a high MICMAC ranking if its development is considered a priori as impossible within the time limit of the study. The variable "climatic changes" is a good example, in that climate can be considered as invariant for a particular study.

Nevertheless, as emphasized, the chief merit of the MICMAC method is its ability to identify a hierarchy of variables that not only serves to confirm some basic intuitions but also, by virtue of its counterintuitive aspects, poses questions that would not otherwise have come to mind.

Finally, it is from among the variables at the head of the MICMAC ranking that the main research priorities will be defined, thus permitting the field of study and the complexity of the system to be confined to the essential variables. This does not prevent others from being adopted even if ranked low by MICMAC.

The explanation of the system by structural analysis highlights its structure, that is, the relationships between dominant (driving or motor) variables and dominated (dependent, sensitive) variables. But it introduces two types of question. First, how are the essential variables (dominant and dominated) likely to develop? Second, taking account of these likelihoods, how will the relationships between these variables take effect? In what direction? With what intensity and what consequences? It is obvious that the answer to these questions is multiple, since the future is subject to degrees of freedom (see Part I) and because the effective realization of one possible future or a different one at a given time will depend on the human actions that the actors in the system undertake between now and then.

The method of scenarios was developed precisely to describe this multiple future and to answer these questions.

5 Scenarios— A Multiple View of An Uncertain Future

The future is multiple and several futures are possible (potential futures); the path leading to this or that future is not necessarily unique. The description of a potential future and of the progression toward it comprises a "scenario." The word scenario was introduced in futurology by H. Kahn several years ago in his book The Year 2000, but here the usage was primarily literary, with the imagination being used to produce a more or less rose-colored or apocalyptic prediction previously attempted by classical authors such as Anatole France (Island of Penguins), George Orwell (1984).

In France it was the Omnium textiles articles ménagers (OTAM, a general trading company) team that, during a prospective study in the field of geography carried out on behalf of the Délégation en aménagement des territoires et action régionale (DATAR), first put into practice the scenarios method (39, 42). This method was subsequently adapted for use in an industrial context, particularly during a prospective study in "chemistry-agriculture" carried out by C. Kintz and G. Ribeill.

At the same time, American researchers Gordon, Elmer Dalkey, and others developed several relatively formalized methods of constructing scenarios, all based on the gathering of expert opinion: Delphi technique, cross-impact matrices, etc. These developments are regularly published in the journals Futures (GB) and Technological Forecasting and Social Change (USA).

Agreement between these two approaches (for convenience called "literary" and "formalized") seems to be difficult to achieve. Defenders of the former vigorously reject mathematical modeling and denounce the hidden ideological meaning (often in the name of another ideology). Proponents of the latter find devoid of interest and verbose anything that does not bear the seal of the computer. The author has had the good fortune to be involved in both approaches: He developed new methods of structural analysis (MICMAC) and of cross-impacts (SMIC 74) (62, 64) and also used the scenarios method (literary) in a prospective study of air transport up to 1990, carried out under the direction of C. Kintz on behalf of Paris Airport. During the air transport study, a need was felt to marry the two approaches, thus providing cross fertilization, with each method serving to contain the excesses of the other.

As a living concept this synthesis is in a permanent state of analysis, development, and improvement. But it is this synthesis of methods and approaches that we propose to present here. First, however, before presenting the "literary" and "formalized" approaches and a synthesis, we will describe in detail the concepts to be used.

DEFINITION OF CONCEPTS

The following concepts will be successively defined:

1. An invariant

2. A trend

3. A germ

4. An actor

5. A strategy

6. Conflicts

7. Events

8. Randomness, subjective probabilities

9. Images and scenarios and

10. Trend-based scenarios and contrasted scenarios.

- An invariant: a phenomenon assumed to be permanent up to the horizon studied. Example: climatic phenomena.

- Strong trend: a movement affecting a phenomenon in such a way that its development in time can be predicted. Example: urbanization.

- A germ: a factor of change hardly perceptible at present, but which will constitute a strong trend in the future. In fact, a germ variable is just what Pierre Massé described as a harbinger of the future: "A sign which is slight in terms of present dimensions but huge in terms of its virtual consequences."

- Actors: those who play an important role in the system through variables which characterize their plans and which they, to some extent, control. Example: the consuming countries, the producing countries, the multi-nationals, etc. are actors in the energy system.

- A strategy: a set of tactics (set of conditional decisions) determining each actor's acts relative to his plan under every possible contingency.

- A conflict: may result from the confrontation between opposing strategies of the actors, and may take the form of an outbreak of tension between two tendencies (overcrowding and lack of space, constrained time and free time...). The outcome of these conflicts determines the evolution of the balance of force between actors, or strengthens the weight of one trend or another.

● An event (see Note 1): the notion of an event is defined by E. Borel (40) in the following manner: "An event is an abstract entity whose only characteristic is to happen or not to happen." An event can be considered as a variable taking only one of two values, in general "1" if the event happens, and "0" if the event does not happen; such an event will be called an isolated event.

● Randomness, subjective probabilities: we refer to the long established but still relevant work of Professor Ville. A phenomenon is said to be random when it can take a certain number of values, to each of which is attached a subjective probability. We "can consider the calculation of the probability of an isolated event as a subjective judgment, insofar as the considered event is classified in a category of events which subjectively have the same degree of probability. It is thus the expert who, in passing his judgment, establishes his categories." (50, p. 139). A subjective probability is a gamble (which is almost always list if we consider an event which will in fact either occur (probability one) or not (probability zero) (see Note 2), but which must be considered as won if, among all the events to which we have attributed X chances in 100 of occurring, there are actually X in 100 which occurred at the given time (see Note 3).

● A scenario: the description of a future situation together with the progression of events leading from the base situation to the future situation (39). It should be added that this set of events should display a certain consistency. This definition is in fact very wide and covers two very different categories of scenario: situational scenarios or images, i.e., the description of future situations, and developmental scenarios, i.e., the different trains of events that lead there. In other words, a developmental scenario is a continuous film of the development of a system, while a situational scenario is a "snapshot."

Furthermore the distinction between a trend-based scenario and a contrasted scenario, traditional as it may be, is not the same for everyone.

● The trend-based scenario corresponds to the most likely course of events at all the decision points, taking account of the tendencies implicit in a starting situation (39, p. 122).

Thus the trend scenario, contrary to what is suggested by its name, does not necessarily correspond to a pure and simple extrapolation of trends. It is the most likely scenario. Certainly, in the recent past, when the world changed less rapidly than today, the most likely development was the continuation of trends. For the future, however, the most likely often appears to entail a clean break with present trends.

The extrapolation of trends can lead to a very contrasted situation, as was shown in a study carried out for DATAR published in Metra under the title "Trend Scenario for France" and for the Documentation Francaise under the title "Scenario of the Unacceptable" (42, 51).

In this case the trend-based scenario consists of extrapolating trends, and not of the most likely course of events (see Note 4). As a result of this study, a certain amount of confusion of language has set in, and we therefore propose to use the term "trend-based scenario" in the sense of the most likely, since this is more current usage (see Note 5).

• The contrasted scenario is "the exploration of a purposely extreme theme, the a priori determination of a future situation" (39). Whereas the trend-based scenario corresponds to an exploratory approach, from a developmental to a situational scenario, the contrasted scenario corresponds to a normative approach; a scenario for a future situation or image is chosen such that it contrasts strongly with the present (coastal France, the France of 100 million inhabitants) from which starting point an investigation is made into the course of events (i.e., the scenario) leading up to it.

Usage has also sanctioned another definition of the contrasted scenario reflecting, like the trend-based scenario, an exploratory attitude, leading via development into a situation. In this case, just as the trend-based scenario is defined as the most likely course of events, the contrasted scenario is defined as a very unlikely course of events, and it is just this general nature, highly contrasted, which makes it unlikely. This is the definition which will henceforth be adopted.

This does not mean that we are abandoning the normative in favor of the exploratory; in our view this distinction is only of operational significance. In fact once the development and the situation have been described one way or another, the approach is both exploratory and normative.

Readers should be reminded of the distinction between possible scenarios, i.e., everything that can be imagined, and realizable scenarios, i.e., everything possible under known constraints. It is among these scenarios, whose probability is not zero, that the contrasted (improbable) scenarios are found and also the core of developments containing the most likely scenarios, particularly the trend-based scenario. The desirable scenarios are found somewhere within the realm of the possible and they are not necessarily all realizable.

THE "LITERARY" APPROACH

It will be recalled that by literary approach we mean a method based entirely on thought and reasoning, excluding all mathematical or computer processes.

The scenarios method was developed to account for the long-term development of complex systems as represented by a company, a sector, or a country, along with their environments.

A study involving the scenarios method comprises two main stages: the construction of the base, and the elaboration of the scenarios.

To present this method, we shall draw on a study carried out recently which set out to define the long-term development strategies (15 years) for a company in the chemical sector. To anticipate the opportunities or pitfalls of modern agricultural developments for this company would allow it to prepare for the changes in its environment. We shall also refer to a prospective study of air transport for the Parisian region.

Construction of the Base

The first stage attempts to construct the "base," i.e., an "image" of the present state of the system, which will serve as a starting point for the prospective study. This image must be

- detailed and comprehensive, both quantitatively and qualitatively.

- broad in scope (economic, technological, political, sociological,...).

- dynamic, bringing out past trends and harbingers of the future.

- explanatory (mechanisms of change) and actors (movers of the system).

The base is constructed in three phases: the delimitation of the system studied, the study of the present situation, and the examination of past development.

Delimitation of the System Studied

This forms an important phase. Care should be taken not to exclude a priori from the field of study those technical, economic, and political elements that are now without influence on the phenomenon studied but which might in the longer term begin to exercise significant influences on the development of the system. For example, to study the food industry, synthetic foodstuffs should not be forgotten. Conversely, one should avoid falling into the trap of carrying out a prospective study for the whole of society, whatever the subject of the actual study.

This phase results in a more precise definition of the system being studied. For example, in a prospective study of the food industry, the system studies included:

human consumption, both quantitative (population) and qualitative (way-of-life) aspects, the food industries, the agricultural system, broken down into arable and livestock rearing, the chemical industries, those aspects of pollution that concern the other elements of the system, national or international political power.

Study of the Present Situation

A prospective study does not take into consideration merely quantified or quantifiable information, but also all qualitative data (economic data, sociological factors, political factors, etc.) that make up the environment of the phenomenon studied. The approach is therefore an over-all one, which attempts to understand the structure of the system by identifying the driving element (trends, germs, mechanisms). This analysis of the system allows the different actors present to be identified, together with the flows, the constraints and the mechanisms that characterize them and condition their strategy. Using the same examples as before, we have:

● The <u>actors of the system</u>: the political power (national and international), the consumer (rural, urban, in cooperative organizations, industrialists, farmers...);

● The <u>flows</u>:   the flow of goods between the chemical industries and agriculture, of agricultural produce, of manufactured products..., the flow of active persons between the agricultural and other sectors (rural exodus);

● The <u>constraints</u>: biological constraints (nutrition), economic constraints (the incomes of farmers and of industrialists, the purchasing power of consumers...), the accessibility to agricultural workers of jobs in industry or in the service sector;

● The <u>controls</u>:   the European Economic Community (EEC) common agricultural policy, industrial integration policy...;

● The <u>mechanism</u>: the effects of population movements on the consumption of food, the incidence of urbanization, price support policies that interfere with the mechanisms regulating production... .

The last stage of the study of the present situation consists of gathering together in a double-entry table the strategies of the different actors present in the system. This type of presentation shows up the potential conflicts that can arise among the actors, as well as the possible alliances.

For example, for a prospective study of air transport, we have constructed a table of strategies including the following actors: builders, companies, state, airport, nearby residents... (see Chapter 6).

Examination of Past Developments

An examination of the development of the system during previous years first of all prevents undue weight being given to the present situation, which could lead to biases caused by temporary factors. An examination of the past also attempts to bring out the structural variables of the system, i.e., the invariants and the major trends, which might be postulated to be constant during the entire period of study.

Among the invariants can be mentioned, in the case of our example, the general economic system, the nutritional requirements of man, the composition of the western diet, etc.... As examples of strong trends can be mentioned the effect of increasing urganization of the population on its food consumption, trends towards communal eating, and, associated with this, the growing use of processed foodstuffs, etc.

Finally, it is useful to try to break down such a complex system into subsystems as autonomous as possible, which can be submitted to separate prospective studies, while still taking into account their mutual interrelationships. These different subsystems are represented by diagrams, which set out the result obtained.

Results

By this stage of the study the important results have already been attained:

1. The system studied is limited to the relevant elements.

2. The system is structured and finally subdivided into subsystems.

3. Its past development and present state are explained (interpreted).

4. The factors of change or of stability of the system are highlighted.

5. The plans of the actors are identified in a strategic table.

Elaboration of Scenarios

The truly prospective part of the study is subdivided into two phases: the elaboration of a trend-based scenario and the elaboration of contrasted scenarios. The period to be studied is broken up into successive subperiods and, within each subperiod, into a diachronous study and a synchronous study.

Subdivision of the Period of Study

In a prospective study, it is very difficult to directly conceive an image of the system studied within the chosen time frame based on the present situation, because this does not allow for changes that affect the system during the course of the period of study. The full time period is therefore split up into shorter subperiods of several years, during each of which the system is assumed to be relatively constant. For example, two subperiods of five years (1973-1978 and 1978-1983) and a subperiod of seven years (1983-1990) were adopted for the prospective study of air transport, with regard to the various degrees of inertia appropriate to this system.

The diachronous study

During the first subperiod, the construction of the basis led to the identification of the invariants, the strong trends, the agents involved, the evolutionary factors of the system. Starting from these elements, and making hypotheses regarding the development of the environment, it is possible to trace the development of the system and of the subsystems during the subperiod.

The synchronous study

At the end of the subperiod, it is useful to reconstitute the base, by gathering together the various elements of the developments described in the diachronous study, so as to ensure the consistency of the different developments and to bring out the changes that have affected the system.

In this way, changes can be detected (1) of structure (for example one agent may have been absorbed by another agent), 2) of mechanisms (it may be thought that the present policy of supporting food prices cannot be maintained because it has a strong tendency to lead to agricultural surpluses, and that replacement by another policy may be necessary) or of 3) modifications in the objectives of the agents (for example because they have achieved their first objectives).

On completion of the synchronous study, a new base is drawn up, and a new diachronous study may be carried out by successive iterations. By alternating diachronous studies with synchronous studies, an image of the system being studied within the chosen time frame is built up.

Elaboration of a Trend-Based Scenario

The trend scenario provides an image of the system studied on the date chosen after the most likely evolution of the system. This means of course that each time there is a crossroads in the development possibilities of the system during its construction, an assumption is made as to the most likely choice.

Elaboration of Contrasted Scenarios

Here we talk about setting limits within which the image of the system may vary. It will be remembered that a scenario is designated trend-based when, confronted with several possible lines of development, the most likely is chosen. For example in a trend-based scenario, it is conceded that in 1986 consumers will still prefer beefsteaks to "petrochemical steaks." On the other hand, by choosing the converse hypothesis, a contrasted scenario is defined.

By making both an optimistic and a pessimistic hypothesis of a parameter, contrasted scenarios that enclose a trend-based scenario can be constructed.

Synthesis of Scenarios and Developmental Strategy

After constructing the trend-based and contrasted scenarios, it is useful to analyze them, distinguishing the possible from the realizable, and presenting to the decision-makers conclusions that will help them select a program of action and adapt the development plan of the country or company to the different possible directions of development of the environment. If, for example, a scenario shows that the consumption of fertilizer will attain a saturation level at a certain time, one strategy for a fertilizer producer might be to content himself with this level of production, but another might also be to further explore this market by offering services as well as the product itself.

The usefulness of a prospective study may extend over several years; as time passes, actual events are compared with the hypotheses underlying each scenario. Insight will thus be gained as to which theoretical past (developmental scenario) corresponds most closely to reality.

This continuous process of the future becoming the present makes it easier to adhere to the path initially anticipated, and allows, if appropriate, corrective measures to be taken.

Knowledge about the "true" path of development of a phenomenon is of prime importance in distinguishing in subsequent events between conjunctural fluctuations and structural changes (for example, in distinguishing between a transitory downturn in sales and a more fundamental crisis in the market).

Conclusions

The different stages of the literary approach fit together and succeed each other according to a logical scheme that has proven its value in the course of numerous prospective studies.

THE FORMALIZED APPROACH

In the same way as structural analysis was developed to appreciate and structure more and more complex systems, the cross-impact methods facilitate the elaboration of scenarios. This is the "formalized" approach.

By formalized approach we mean a method that draws primarily on mathematical and data processing methods to make use of the available information. Social systems are becoming more and more complex and diversified, phenomena more and more interdependent, events more and more related. As a result, control over the future depends increasingly on early knowledge of what the future holds in store.

In the same way as history can be summarized in terms of a number of crucial events, possible futures may be identified by a list of events that, if they occur, are considered important at a given time. This set of events comprises a frame of reference within which there are as many possible states (potential futures) as there are combinations of events. It was to determine the most likely events, and thus scenarios, that formalized methods known as cross-impact matrices began to be developed from 1968.

The Object of Cross-Impact Methods

Often the only information relating to events that might occur in the future and that would influence the phenomena we are seeking to forecast takes the form of personal judgment.

Some methods, such as Delphi techniques, are well suited to collecting opinions and producing a convergent result. But this method has the defect of not taking into account the interactions between events. Conversely the cross-impact method (MIC, after the French Méthode des Impacts Croisés) has the advantage of taking account both of opinions expressed and of interdependencies between questions, therefore providing a more consistent frame of reference. The cross-impact method is the generic term for a family of techniques that attempt to evaluate changes in the probabilities of occurrence of a set of events following the occurrence of one of them. This method appears, first of all, as a list of events with probabilities of occurrence associated with them: The basic hypothesis underlying the method is that the elementary probabilities take account of the interactions, but only incompletely. By taking account of the interdependencies between events, we can move from a system of raw probabilities to a system of net, or corrected, probabilities.

The next stage of the method consists of analyzing the sensitivity of the system to events, and also of constructing scenarios.

Sensitivity analysis allows the motor (or dominant) events and the dominated events to be identified. This usually involves estimating the variations ΔP_j of the probability P_j of the event j following a variation ΔP_i in the probability P_i of event i. The results take the form of an elasticity matrix shown in Fig. 5.1

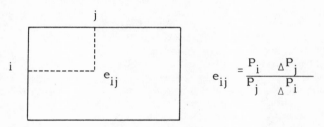

Fig. 5.1   Elasticity Matrix

The elaboration of scenarios is usually carried out by random sampling procedures, which, except for two methods recently developed, allow the most probable chain of events to be generated.

If we consider a system of N events $(e_1, e_2, ..., e_N)$, there are 2^N states or situational scenarios possible for this system.

For example, to say that at a certain date, events $e_1, e_2, e_4, ..., e_N$ will occur, and not e_3, is one of these 2^N scenarios. We will see that only two methods give the probabilities of all the situational scenarios.

If account is taken of the order in which the events occur, there are $N!2^N$ development scenarios.

Brief Historical Survey

Several cross-impact methods have been proposed. First of all, with Gordon in 1968 (47), the evaluation of interactions was carried out by means of impact coefficients between +10 and -10, the transition from raw probabilities usually making use of rather sophisticated techniques (Monte Carlo methods with successive repetitions).

The work of Howard and Johnson in 1970 (48) and of Julius Kane in 1972-73 (50) continued along the methodological lines established by Gordon and continued to mix the impact coefficients with the probabilities in the transition from raw to net probabilities.

Following the work of Gordon, other approaches were taken. Norman Dalkey (41) introduced a conditional probability matrix between all pairs of events in order to modify the system of initial probabilities. This approach, which marks an advance on the MIC suggested by Gordon and improved by Dalkey, nevertheless has a low credibility. The results obtained, in fact, depend on the formula adopted for converting to net probabilities.

Several different approaches were proposed, often comprising a judicious mix of quadratic forms, mathematical expectancies, and subjective weighting coefficients. In practice, none of the methods prevailed over the others and in a single example, as shown by Florentin and Isaac-Dognin (45), there may be as many results as formulas tested. Furthermore, use of the transformation formula $P_i(1-P_i)$, which gives a maximum of $P_i = 0.5$ and a minimum for $P_i = 0$ or 1, is not at all justified. This method tends to limit the corrections for gross probabilities close to 0.5 and to facilitate those for the extreme probabilities.

The concern to suggest a meaningful transformation formula led authors such as Enzer to appeal to information theory. This approach is attractive, but the calculation of results remains complex and rather subjective (the use of individual and collective weighting coefficients). The objective of the method should be to ensure the consistency of the estimates relative to the classical constraints on the probabilities.

In practice, most of the methods, whatever their degree of complexity, lead to inconsistent net probabilities, with results such as the following: $P(i) < P(i/j)$. $P(j)$, which is not compatible with the relationship $P(i) = P(i/j)P(j)+P(i/j')$. $p(J')$ which should always be checked. The American authors confuse convergence with consistency. The fact that a process is convergent does not necessarily imply that the results obtained are consistent. This remark is also valid for the Delphi technique.

Recent Developments

The principal work is that of Duval, Fontela and Gabus at the Battelle Institute in Geneva (43, 46) and the Markovian model of J. Eymard (44) (Paris Airport), developed following the application of the SMIC 74 method to the prospective study of air transport, a method developed by the author with J. C. Duperrin (63).

TABLE 5.1 Comparative Cross-Impact Matrix

Methods	Characteristics					
	Homogenity of elements	Search for coherence in proba-bility	Formula to move from gross to net probability	Sensitivity analysis	Elaboration of scenarios	Probability of situation-al scenarios
Gordon, 1968 (47)	No	No	Yes	Yes	No	No
Howard and John-son 1970 (48)	No	No	Yes	Yes	Yes	No
Julius Kane 1972/3 (50)	No	No	Yes	Yes	No	No
Dalkey (41)	Yes	No	Yes	Yes	Yes	No
Battelle, 1972	Yes	Yes	Yes, but no solution	No	No	No
Battelle, 1974 (43)	Yes	Insufficient	No	No	Yes, the most likely scenario	No
SMIC (63)	Yes	Yes	Yes	Yes	Yes, all possi-ble scenarios	Yes
J. Eymard Markovian Model	No	No	No	Yes, indirectly	Yes, all possi-ble scenarios	Yes

The Battelle Method

The Battelle and SMIC methods have common features in that they both work with homogeneous data (only probabilities), they both seek consistent results, and they develop scenarios. But the similarity stops there.

It appears that since their work in 1972 the Battelle researchers have abandoned the solution that consisted of minimizing a certain function of individual and conditioned probabilities subject to constraints of types a, b, and c. (See p. 62). In fact the nonlinearity of the constraints led to almost insoluble problems in seeking the optimum.

The present solution (46, pp. 47, 48) consists of only asking the experts about certain probabilities. For example, to calculate $P(i/j')$ taking into account c, it is sufficient to know $p(i/j)$. Although this practice has the advantage of constructing a consistent matrix, relative to otherwise insufficient constraints, it has the grave defect for example of considering the estimate $P(i/j)$ precise and the opinion of the expert or group of experts as perfect.

In addition, the Battelle method determines the most likely chain of events by the classical process of random sampling.

In this connection, the reader is reminded that for a system of N events, there are 2^N states possible, and that the sum of the probabilities of the scenarios is equal to one, since these situational scenarios are mutually exclusive, and one of them must occur. As has been shown in the cases where SMIC has been used, not only does the most likely scenario usually have a probability of the order of 0.2, but in general there are other, totally different scenarios, which have only slightly lower probability, and which must be considered.

Both the Battelle research workers and the American authors missed this phenomenon, since the methods they employed do not give the hierarchical sequence of all the possible scenarios, unlike the SMIC method and the Markovian model of J. Eymard.

The Markovian Model of J. Eymard (44)

As suggested by its name, this cross-impact method is based on a Markov matrix, i.e., a matrix of probabilities of transition from one state to another. The innovation of this method, with respect to the others, is in providing the probabilities of all the developmental scenarios and therefore of the situational ones. Thus, not only does this method give the probabilities of situational scenarios at a given horizon, but it also specifies the order in which the events occur. (For N events, there are 2^N situational scenarios, corresponding to $N!2^N$ scenarios of possible development.)

Nevertheless, what we gain on the swings we lose on the roundabouts. Although this method is the one that presents the most complete results in regard to scenarios, three criticisms can be made of it:

1. It does not lend itself directly to a sensitivity analysis.

2. In view of the number of questions to be put to the experts, more than five events can hardly be taken into account.

3. There is no check on the statistical consistency of the starting probabilities, which is no better than in other cases.

SMIC Method (Systems and Cross-Impact Matrix (63, 68)

The principle underlying the method is extremely simple and is based on the assumption that the experts consulted are able to give opinions on the three concerns itemized below.

1. The list H of the n hypotheses (or events) considered relevant to the exercise in hand:

$$H = (e_1, e_2, ..., e_n)$$

2. The probability $P(i)$ of the hypothesis e_1 (i.e., the probability of the occurrence of e_i within the period considered).

3. The conditional probabilities of the hypotheses taken in pairs:

$P(i/j)$ is the probability of i if j occurs.

$P(i/j')$ is the probability of i if j does not occur.

In practice, the opinions given in response to certain specific questions about nonindependent hypotheses disclose some degree of inconsistency with the over-all opinion (implicit, not expressed) revealed by the answers given to all the other questions. These "raw" opinions thus have to be corrected so that the "finished" probabilities conform with the following constraints:

a) $0 < P(i) < 1$.

b) $P(i/j) P(j) = P(j/i) P(i) = P(ij)$.

c) $P(i/j) P(j) + P(i/j') P(j') = P(i)$.

Objectives and Principles of the Method

The method is designed to enable experts' estimates to be checked for consistency against the constraints above. The idea behind it is that each item of information contributed by the experts allows (but only incompletely) for interactions between hypotheses, Consequently, the estimates need to be corrected and the modus operandi for converting them into "finished" form must be based on an objective rule, i.e., one that expresses the agreement of the estimates with the constraints imposed.

One approach might have been to optimize a given factor of the individual and conditional probabilities by reference to those constraints, but the nonlinear character of constraints on the probability of the hypotheses means that special conditions would have to be observed with respect to the optimum. Consequently, we investigated the probability ratings of the different possible images of the whole system made up by the hypotheses.

If we characterize the possibilities of development of the problem studied by the realization or not of N fundamental hypotheses (in general 5 or 6), we obtain 2^N sets of hypotheses of 2^N possible images or situational scenarios. If N = 2, we have two hypotheses H1 and H2 and four possible scenarios:

H1 and H2 realized
H1 realized, H2 not realized
H1 not realized, H2 realized
H1 and H2 not realized

The principle we adopted was to strive toward a consistent and complete "finished product" by considering the probabilities of scenarios, i.e., combinations of hypotheses. This is illustrated in Fig. 5-2.

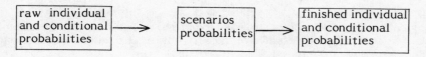

Fig. 5.2   "Raw" and "Finished" Probabilities

Objective Function

Constraints a, b, and c are obeyed by the theoretical probability rating, but the personal estimates of experts do not obey these constraints. Consequently, the objective function we propose to optimize is one that minimizes the difference between the $p(i/j)\ p(j)$ resulting from the experts' conclusions and the theoretical $*(i/j)\ P*(j)$ factors expressed in terms of π_k. This means that we must determine the probabilities $(\pi_1, \pi_2, ..., \pi_k, \pi_r)$ of the "r" possible scenarios that minimize an objective function.
Subject to the constraints:

$$\sum_{k=1}^{r} \pi_k = 1, \quad \pi_k \geq 0 \text{ for all k.}$$

This is a classic minimization problem of quadratic form with linear constraints (see Note 6).

Results: Ranking Scenarios and Sensitivity Analysis

The computer program output gives us the probability rating for the "r" possible images or situational scenarios $(\pi_1, \pi_2, \pi_{.j}, ..., \pi_r)$. By this means we achieve a cardinal ranking of the possible images and can thus circumscribe the area of plausible developments by retaining only those scenarios with a probability greater than zero.
The trend-based or reference scenario and the contrasted scenario are chosen among the most probable images.
From the probabilities of scenarios we can calculate the finished probabilities of the hypotheses that are not only consistent with the experts' predictions but also consonant with the probability constraints.
The next step in the method consists of an analysis of the sensitivity of the system of hypotheses. An important part of this analysis is estimating the variation $P_{(j)}$ of $P_{(j)}$ consequent on a variation $P_{(i)}$ of $P_{(i)}$.

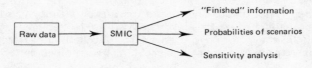

Fig. 5.3   Raw Data SMIC

Conclusion

As shown in Fig. 5-3, SMIC systematically takes account of the opinions expressed by experts and of the interdependencies between the questions asked. It lends itself well to sensitivity analysis.

Not only does SMIC correct raw information in order to give <u>consistent results</u> for the probabilities of hypotheses, but it also gives the <u>scenario probabilities</u>, and permits the identification from within the class of realizable scenarios, the <u>most likely situational scenarios</u>.

SMIC, 1976 Version

Several criticisms can be levelled against SMIC, at least as originally used, relating to:

- its overmechanical and limited application,
- the objective function and the multiplicity of solutions.
- the problem of aggregating the replies of a number of experts.

Each of these three points is worth further consideration.

Overmechanical and Limited Application

The introduction of a new technique is followed by a period of familiarization during which there is a tendency to use it for the fun of it, as an end in itself. In the case of SMIC this period was brief, and the method is now used only with great restraint, within the framework of the integrated approach.

The number of hypotheses SMIC can deal with is generally limited to six, not so much for mathematical reasons as for the number of questions the experts can reasonably cope with. Six hypotheses require 66 questions, but seven require 91.

The Objective Function and the Multiplicity of Solutions

First of all, the objective function is to some extent arbitrary. Another could have been chosen. Nevertheless the objective function adopted has the merit of consistency with the "philosophy" of least squares.

As for linear regression, we are given an array of points (the raw replies) and we seek the closest possible information that obeys certain constraints (the straight line "or regression," the axioms of probability in our case). Furthermore it is correct, as was shown by Mitchell and Tydeman (66), and also by the author himself two years ago (67), that the optimum of this objective function is not unique and indeed there is an infinity of solutions for the scenario probabilities π_k. Nevertheless, as is demonstrated in the author's reply (68), the solution presented by Mitchell and Tydeman is an impasse, and it is proposed that this problem be resolved by an improved version of SMIC.

The 1976 version of SMIC introduces a criterion of choice, and the solution actually adopted from among the infinity of solutions is the one that gives the highest possible value to the most likely scenario. The solution meeting this criterion, i.e., $\max_k \{\max \pi k\}$ may easily be obtained by the simplex method. This criterion has the advantage of partly removing a contradiction often noted between the results of SMIC (which in general gives a rather low probability to the most likely scenario) and the initial point of view of the expert interviewed, according to whom one or two scenarios are distinctly more likely than the others.

The Problem of Aggregating Replies

In view of the computing costs, it would not be practicable to apply SMIC separately in respect to each of the experts involved. Furthermore this would lead to the emergence of as many solutions as there are experts, and a choice would sooner or later be necessary.

The solution we suggest, as illustrated by an example in Chapter 7, is to construct a typology of experts according to their replies, and to ultimately adopt the scenarios that seem the most likely for the largest number of experts considered as types, i.e., representatives of categories.

CONCLUSION

The world in which we live is based on such a complex web of interdependent relationships that it is difficult to observe the behavior of a system without envisaging the influences it undergoes and the impacts it produces. Each system must therefore be placed in a wider context, taking into account sociopolitical as well as technological aspects to obtain as full a picture as possible of a given time frame.

The human mind is unable to grasp the totality of relationships between nonindependent elements, and therefore usually restricts itself to binary comparisons. The "formalized approach," using cross-impact methods, is one of the tools of the prospective approach best adapted to help assimilate the complex web of interactions. To understand the transformation of a system, it is not sufficient to identify certain distinctive events; the probabilities of the corresponding scenarios must also be known.

SMIC actually gives a sequence of the most likely possible futures. The principle of this new cross-impact method consists of correcting the opinions expressed by the experts, taking account of the interdependencies between the questions asked, and constructing from the probabilities associated with pairs of hypotheses a consistent set of scenario probabilities.

Sensitivity analysis shows that this method allows the impact of an action on a variable to be assessed, and thus, a strategy to be chosen from among the political alternatives by the decision-maker. This allowance for external effects is related to the preoccupations of "Technology Assessment." SMIC has been used in prospective applications in fields as diverse as nuclear energy, air transport, hydrogen, and international relations.

The role played by creativity in such a method should be emphasized. While 80-90% of the results are such as to be immediately grasped intuitively, 10% of the results are counterintuitive and pose questions that would not otherwise have come to mind.

This new cross-impact method does not, however, any more than any other methodology, consistute a panacea. Whatever the system studied, the choice of variables and relationships depends on the value-system of the experts questioned. We should therefore be aware of the danger of manipulation in such methods, in which the initial hypotheses condition the result so strongly. The value of the formalized approach lies not in replacing the role of the human mind, but in its ability to guide thought and enrich analysis, while at the same time providing a cross-check on the literary approach.

While SMIC seems to be one of the best in terms of performance, its current form is not the final one, and further constructive criticism will undoubtedly give rise to new improvements in the future. As a general conclusion to this second part, we propose a synthesis of methods and approaches.

6 The Two-Scenario Method An Integrated Approach

The different methods that have been discussed here, structural analysis (MICMAC) and cross-impacts (SMIC), although capable of being used independently of each other, also lend themselves perfectly to sequential application. The formalization and synthesis of this approach into a single methodological development is best appreciated when carried out along the lines of the logical development of the literary approach. This synthesis of approaches is the subject of this chapter, which describes the method of scenarios actually in use by SEMA.

INTRODUCTION - SCENARIOS METHOD IN AN UNCERTAIN FUTURE

Most forecasting methods rely on the extrapolation of trends, on an "all other things being equal" reasoning that can now be seen to be illusory in an environment undergoing changes and where the phenomena to be taken into account are increasingly complex and interdependent. In such methods the uncertainty in regard to the future is reflected in the form of divergencies about a trend (upper and lower limits).

Such econometric models, however, have been found to be powerless when the forecasting of structural change (crises) is involved and where users attribute forecasting errors to the famous "hidden" variables.

The prospective approach, by contrast, accepts that today the future is multiple, and that it is the confrontation between the various actors involved and their projects that give rise to one future or another. The construction of the future is explained as much by human action as deterministic factors.

The scenarios method is concerned with deriving these multiple futures and with exploring the pathways leading to them. Literary scenarios, however, while they may represent a stimulating exercise for the imagination, necessarily suffer from lack of credibility since it is impossible to verify the validity and plausibility of the hypotheses advanced. This is why

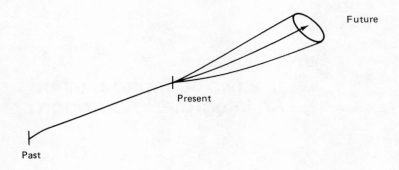

Fig. 6.1 The future is unique and certain

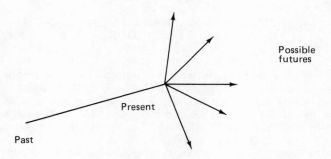

Fig. 6.2 The future is multiple and undetermined

we at SEMA have developed an integrated prospective approach that in particular shows:

1. that variables are frequently hidden only to the models. The use of structural analysis makes it possible to reveal them and to demonstrate the roles they play.

2. that it is possible, using a method of cross impacts, to rank the scenarios on the basis of their probability.

The objectives of such a method are:

● To identify which points should be studied as a matter of priority (key-variables), by confronting the variables relating to the phenomenon being studied with the variables describing the environment, and by using the over-all explanatory analysis that is as exhaustive as possible.

● To determine, particularly in relation to the key variables, the fundamental actors, their strategies, and the resources at their disposal to achieve their objectives and the constraints they must overcome. This is the specific object of the retrospective and immediate analysis.

Describing in the form of scenarios the most probable development of the phenomena studied, based on the most likely development of the variables, with hypotheses about the behavior of the actors, makes possible the identification of potential futures.

The reader will recall that scenarios describe, on the one hand, the most probable situation of the phenomenon studied and its environment at the end of the time frame, together with the pathways leading to it (reference or trend-based scenario), and, on the other hand, the extreme situations within which this phenomenon will be situated (contrasted scenarios, pessimistic and optimistic). At this point the classical forecasting techniques can be used, within the framework defined by a scenario, to translate the scenario into quantitative terms. It is also possible, by taking into account the various scenarios, to evaluate the consequence of decisions already taken and, with the assistance of multicriteria methods, to deduce the strategic actions that should be taken as a matter of priority to profit to the greatest extent from the expected changes and the contraints likely to be imposed.

THE INTEGRATED APPROACH

The proposed synthesis consists of marrying the formalized and literary approaches so that there will no longer be method without reasoning or reasoning without method. This is the integrated approach which links together the logical and methodological developments: The "literary" approach is concerned with the construction of scenarios by a process of thinking and reasoning. The "formalized" approach nourishes the process of thought about scenarios and allows their validity to be verified. The integrated approach comprises two phases: the construction of the base and the elaboration of scenarios using this base as starting point. In describing this method, we consider the example of the French economy in relation to the external world, but we could also use an enterprise or a sector vis-à-vis a given environment.

Construction of the Base

Construction of the base involves three stages:

- delimitation of the system consisting of France and its environment,
- detemination of the essential variables,
- explanatory analysis of the role played by these variables.

Delimitation of the System

One begins by delimiting the system consisting of France and the outside world. To do this one uses the techniques of structural analysis and defines a certain number of quantifiable or nonquantifiable variables characterizing the system, which can be divided into national variables and external variables. Finally all the direct relationships between external and national variables are entered in a matrix, which represents, to some extent, the structure of the system.

Determination of the Essential Variables

In addition to the direct relationships, there are also indirect relationships between variables involving changes of influence and feedback loops. A normal matrix with several dozen variables can involve several millions of interactions in the form of chains and feedback links. It is impossible at a human level to represent and to interpret such a network of relationships. More detailed exploitation of the matrix of structural analysis, particularly by using the MICMAC method, makes it possible to identify the indirect relationships and the feedback effects between variables and so supplies two types of results:

1. a classification of the national variables as a function of their sensitivity to the exterior (dependent variables),
2. a classification of the external variables as a function of their impact on national variables (motor variables).

MICMAC provides a ranking of the variables. Cartain of these variables will confirm initial intuitions, but others, more surprising, will make it necessary to ask questions not previously asked.

Explanatory Analysis of Role Played by Variables

The explanatory analysis relates the group of essential variables, as identified by the MICMAC treatment. It consists of a retrospective analysis and an analysis of the present situation.

- The retrospective analysis avoid placing exaggerated importance on the present situation, the study of which could be biased by temporary economic factors. The object is to understand the mechanisms and the determinant actors with respect to external and national developments. The object is also used to demonstrate the invariants of the system and the underlying major trends.

- Analysis of the existing situation makes it possible to identify the first stirrings of change in world geopolitical development, together with the strategies of the actors at the origin of this change. To this end this analysis does not only take into consideration quantified or quantifiable information but also all qualitative data such as economic data, sociological factors, political factors, etc. This analysis results, at the end of this stage, in the construction of a table of "strategies of the actors." In practice it is the confrontation of the projects of the actors and the resulting deployment in the balance of power that determine the future.

Elaboration of the Scenarios

Taking into account the motor factors, the strategies of the actors, and the germs of change identified in the previous phases, one then uses the method of scenarios by looking at the mechanisms of change and by confronting the strategies of the actors (possible alliances and conflicts). In this way the various relationships of power between the actors make construction of the scenarios possible. However, since certain determinant factors in respect to the future are uncertain, in particular the result of possible conflicts, it is necessary to make certain hypotheses in respect to these. These hypotheses are then ranked by probability, on the basis of the opinion of experts, and then run through the SMIC method. For each of these hypotheses there exists a scenario one can construct and the implemantation of which is more or less probable. The results of the SMIC method appear in the form of the probability of situation scenarios (combination of hypotheses). They lend themselves to two different uses.

1. They can help to clarify the choice of sets of hypotheses suitable at various points during the logical development of the literary approach. If, for example, SMIC uses geopolitical variables, the most likely set of hypotheses can be adopted (united Europe, OPEC solidarity, etc...), for the reference scenario of the French economy.

2. They can be compared with the results of the elaboration of scenarios obtained logically by the literary approach. Each approach thus serves as

a check on the other, by bringing out a certain number of contradictions that must be resolved, and that might not otherwise have been noticed. This is exactly what was done in the prospective study of air transport in the Paris region (see Chapter 7). It should be noted that in the first case above, the cross-impact method must be carried out at the beginning of the elaboration of scenarios (for the choice of sets of hypotheses), while in the second case the two approaches are developed in parallel. The first case will be called "orientation SMIC" and the second "cross-check SMIC."

Thus the result of the scenarios method consists of:

● on the one hand, a reference scenario corresponding to the most likely set of hypotheses regarding the changes that might occur in the wider system of the French economy during the period studied.

● on the other, contrasted scenarios that set the limits within which the circumstances of this wider system may vary. In principle this would be one optimistic scenario and one pessimistic scenario made up of consistent but rather unlikely sets of political, economic, and technological hypotheses, which are favorable and unfavorable, respectively, for the national economy. The foregoing description can be summarized by Fig. 6-3, in which the literary and formalized approaches are closely combined into a single integrated approach.

STRATEGIES AND DECISION-MAKING

The results of the foregoing phases appear in the form of developmental scenarios in respect to the phenomenon studied (the national economy or an enterprise). This exploratory phase is complemented by a normative phase, in which the consequences of these scenarios are studied for the benefit of decision-makers.

The next stage consists of defining a development strategy, i.e., of building up an estimate of the resources to be mobilized and the actions to be undertaken to achieve the objectives set.

A strategy is constructed from a set of actions so that:

● their consequences in the short, medium, and long term do not conflict with the objectives but, on the contrary, reinforce their achievement. They are mutually consistent.

● at any moment the cluster of actions to be taken is consistent with the requirements of a changing environment.

This last point is fundamental. While it may be relatively easy to define a strategy that today seems well suited to the present situation, one must always be ready to adapt it to take account of changes in the external or even internal situation. It may be that the modifications are slight and that the necessary change of course can be effected by minor adjustments of the sails (conjunctural actions). But on the other hand, these modifications may

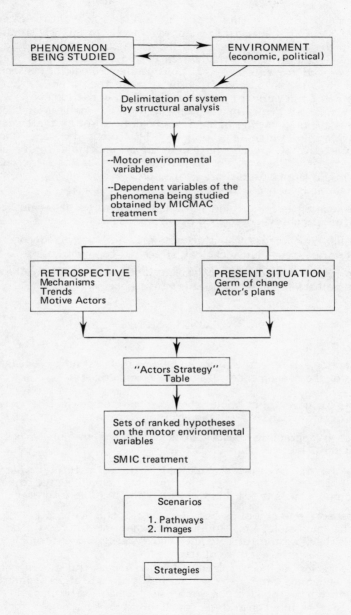

Fig. 6.3. The scenarios method.

require a reappraisal of earlier decisions, or that a new cluster of actions be established (structural actions) to adapt effectively to the new situation.

Thus, in the case of an enterprise, these actions must be directed toward 1) encouraging the effective realization of the scenarios most favorable to the objectives of the enterprise, 2) limiting the prejudicial consequences of the pessimistic scenario, and 3) ensuring that the future activity of the enterprise will fit in well with a constantly evolving environment.

The multiplicity of possible actions creates the problem of choosing the course most judicious in the light of the objectives set by the enterprise and the constraints to which it is subject. SEMA has developed methods of solving problems of choice that arise in an uncertain future and under multiple criteria. The works of B. Roy, in particular the numerous articles published in the journal Metra, are instructive.

These methods allow:

- the consequences of each possible action to be evaluated in the different contexts described by the scenarios.

- each action to be judged according to the criteria important to the enterprise (financial, technical, strategic, commercial, etc.).

- the retention of clusters of priority actions according to the degree of the probable emergence of alternate scenarios.

CONCLUSION

In order for a prospective study to be genuinely useful to decision-making, regardless of the phenomenon examined, it is necessary:

1. that it cover the whole phenomenon studied and its environment (structural analysis assists in ensuring this over-all vision).

2. that it appreciate the dynamics of the system being considered (the MICMAC method helps to do this).

3. finally, that it provide a multiple vision of a future, which is in all respects uncertain (scenarios method, supplemented by the SMIC method, makes it possible to identify the possible futures).

A prospective method cannot, however sophisticated, be expected to achieve the impossible, i.e., to describe what the future will be. Nothing can do this, because the future comes about partly in a deterministic manner and partly through the exercise of free will.

The scenarios method can, however, be a powerful aid to constructive reflection about the future. It can, and this is already of great interest, make it possible to choose with the greatest number of trumps in hand, the strategy that within constraints of all kinds is best suited to attain the objectives set by decision-makers.

III

Concrete Examples of
the Prospective Method

Introduction—
The Two-Scenario Method in
An Uncertain Future

In this part we shall present two case studies of the prospective approach, one relating to air transport and the other to energy.

The use of the SMIC method for a prospective study of air transport in the Paris region up to 1990, carried out on behalf of Paris Airport, is very close to that proposed in the integrated approach (Chapter 6). It included both an "orientation SMIC," which, starting from a table of "actors' strategies," established hypotheses as to the development of the balance of forces between the actors in the air transport system up to 1983, and a "cross-check SMIC" of more traditional scenarios for air transport up to 1990, so as to compare the results of the first with those derived by logical classical reasoning.

The energy study is too recent, however, to allow us to present the approach and results completely, and we shall limit ourselves to presenting the results of SMIC. It should be noted that this study did not make use of structural analysis to delimit the system and identify the essential variables. This must await the prospective study of the global problem (carried out on behalf of a sovereign government) and a prospective study of offshore oil in order to fully demonstrate the integrated approach we suggest. These studies completed in 1976 are even more strategic than the preceding one, and the normal requirements of confidentiality prevent us from divulging most of the results. Consequently in Chapter 8 we propose to give just the briefest results to illustrate the use of "retrospection" and how the SMIC method permits us to choose, cross-check, and contrast scenarios.

7 Air Transport Scenarios for the Paris Region Up to 1990

This study was carried out in 1974 on behalf of Paris Airport. Some of the qualitative results will be presented below, without the corresponding calculations provided to Paris Airport.

First, the contrast scenarios, i.e., optimistic and pessimistic, for air transport were presented. In this connection it should be emphasized that the trend-based scenario, i.e. the most likely, was closer to the pessimistic than the optimistic contrast scenario.

Two applications of the SMIC method were made:

- an orientation SMIC relating to the development in the balance of forces between actors in air transport, which partly helped us to choose the sets of hypotheses necessary to develop the trend-based and contrast scenarios.

- a "cross-check" SMIC on the actual development of air transport (passenger traffic, air traffic control, fares, etc.), the results of which were compared with those from the trend-based and contrast scenarios, thus providing a test of consistency and leading us to ask additional questions.

Only the first application will be presented, as the second has already been published (65).

THE CONTRASTED SCENARIOS

The trend-based scenario provided a mean projection of the possible situation in air transport in the year 1990. We considered it useful to set this projection within two other scenarios, one optimistic and the other pessimistic to provide greater contrast.

Pessimistic Scenario

This scenario is influenced by a set of internally consistent environmental hypotheses that are unfavorable to air transport.

The Geopolitical Background

The world is divided into two spheres of influence controlled by the United States and the Soviet Union, both in the first phase 1974-1980, and in the second. This geopolitical background means that:

- Europe will not emerge as a political entity during the 1980s but will remain simply an enlarged free-trading zone.

- There will be no major conflict. In contrast with the cold war of the 1950s, the United States and the Soviet Union maintain a balance of understanding, although not to the exclusion of local conflicts, particularly in the Middle East, Southeast Asia, and Africa, where the control of natural resources is at stake.

- Fossil fuel costs will rise.

- The growth of American multinationals throughout the world, with their massive foreign investments, will be reflected in an increasing deficit in the American balance of payments.

- The international monetary system will reflect American domination of the western world. The creation of an international monetary standard is controlled by the United States, which uses this device to finance the deficit in its balance of payments. The resulting movement of floating capital provides a strong stimulus to inflation.

- No common transport policy on a European level will emerge, but the possibility exists of relative economy of fossil fuels in European ground transport.

National Economic Background

- Mean growth rate of GNP below 4% throughout the entire period.

- Greater inequalities in income distribution; "stagflation" benefiting the rich.

- Increasing and concentrated urbanization.

- Maintenance of the present work week.

- Deterioration in the amenities (transport, housing); leisure as a time for recuperation.

- The absence of any large-scale political plans (Europe), erosion of the traditional system of values, and deterioration in the amenities as indications of what may be termed a crisis of civilization. Conflicts between social groups more and more vigorous and tense.

- The development of marginal groups.

Consequences for Air Transport

1. Aeronautical construction

As the Americanization and multinationalization spreads, the European construction firms become, at best, subsidiaries. The absence of competition allows the Americans to exploit fully the whole range of existing aircraft without the need, before the end of the 1980s, to introduce a new generation of giant aircraft (1000 seats), which would in any case be badly adapted to a slow-growing market. The "small" aircraft, such as the Boeing 707, are normalized and maintained in service after 1978. A certain levelling up of aircraft toward the top of the existing range can be observed.

2. The airlines

Harmonization of the construction firms' plans facilitates the standardization of the airline fleets. This accords with their need for profitability. The European and American companies agree not to continue transporting seven million empty seats over the North Atlantic. The absence of political unity in Europe prevents the creation of a European airline. In the context of low market growth, the national companies compete vigorously and seek to develop new activities. Air Inter (the major domestic French airline) and smaller airlines of the third level branch out into international routes, Air France attacks the internal market, Paris Airport partly loses its role as a transit center.

3. Passenger traffic

The tourist market stagnates, but the traditional business clientele remains. Analysis of the national situation up to 1990 shows that air transport is developing in a market unfavorable to it. Several factors are responsible for this development:

● Increasing inequality of income distribution, in the context of a low rate of economic growth, does not increase the potential clientele for air transport.

● The constraints that affect lifestyles work in the same direction.

● Growth in tourist traffic is irregular because of spiraling inflation.

● American tourism diminishes because of unsatisfactory reception by Europeans who suffer from a colonial complex.

All of these factors allow a portrait to be sketched of the type of client who avoids air transport: He is a young executive between 25 and 35 years of age. Social success and his standard of living are achieved and maintained at the cost of heavy work pressure. The executive devotes his free time to his wife and children to try to build a normal family life. In particular, long weekends and the annual holidays are spent with his family. Even if the couple would like to travel abroad by air, they have to get over the problem of the children. These constraints are all the more acute since couples are getting married at a younger age and the grandparents, still active, are not always available. In his work the development of telecommunications technology limits his need for traveling.

In the same way the portrait of the stereotype airline traveler may be drawn: Air transport remains expensive and is reserved for a privileged clientele, both tourists and those who travel on business, such as senior executives - in any case less than 5% of the population. Confronted with this situation of low growth in the tourist market, the travel industry is obliged to reconstruct itself. There is a concentration of tour operators who are better placed to bargain with the airlines, particularly since there is no European airline. This concentration is accompanied by a diversification of their services in order to meet the needs of a clientele that is well aware of and demands the ultimate advantages of the other forms of transport (Europe with its surface-transport system).

With short- and medium-haul transport threatened in particular, the tour operators develop their long-haul activities.

Table 7-1 gives traffic forecasts for the pessimistic scenario.

TABLE 7.1 Structural Evolution and Forecasts to 1990

Density of Traffic in France and between France and Selected Points	1960 %	1972 %	1990 %	Total Passengers 1990 (in millions)
Metropolitan France	9	28	20	13
Europe-London	38	36	24	15
London	21	12	6	4
French-speaking Black Africa	15	6	11	7
Other Africa	5	4	6	4
North America	9	10	17	11
South America	1	1	3	2
Far East	2	4	13	8

The results of the trend-based scenario predict 79 million passengers in 1990, the bulk (i.e., 60%) tourists, of whom about 35% would be middle-rank executives (i.e., about 20% of the total traffic). In the pessimistic scenario it is the middle executives who defect from air transport. By reducing by 20% the result of the trend scenario, it can be said broadly that the passenger traffic in the year 1990 will be of the order of 64 millions, corresponding to a mean rate of growth of 8% throughout the period 1972-1990, always of course on the pessimistic assumption.

4. Freight traffic

The structure of foreign trade is strongly influenced by the technological and economic strength of the United States. It is more a case of trade between multinational firms than between particular countries. The countries in possession of the resources are able to carry out industrialization only with American aid.

Compared with the trend-based scenario, the development of trade between Europe and the newly enriched countries is limited, since particular states extend fewer privileges to each other, and Europe loses power and prestige in the Third World.

The growth of freight traffic is less than expected. Furthermore the widespread existence of large-capacity general-purpose aircraft provides a cheap transportation capability that competes strongly with the development of cargo aircraft. The scope for cargo aircraft would be over the North Atlantic, provided there were no container shipping. By contrast with the trend-based scenario, the ratio of imports to exports by air continues to deteriorate.

5. The situation for Paris Airport

In a situation of minimal traffic growth, Paris Airport would not encounter any difficulties from the European airlines that have not managed to structure themselves at a European level. Insofar as Paris Airport has associated itself with the concentration of tour operators, it might even influence the formulation of airline policy by favoring the development of charters and by participating in the improvement of service. However, Paris Airport might encounter certain difficulties in regard to freight if it were to be carried largely by general-purpose aircraft and unloaded onto passenger platforms not constructed for this purpose. The problem of underutilization of the freight area would arise. Growing urbanization around the airports and the fact that air transport serves only a minority lead to the development of protest movements by nearby residents, who demand less noisy aircraft and the closing of airports at night.

The Optimistic Scenario

This scenario is based on environmental assumptions that are compatible with each other and have characteristics favorable to air transport.

The Geopolitical Background

This scenario is based on a world of five blocs: The United States, the Soviet Union, Japan and China, Europe, and the rest of the world (Africa, Middle East, etc.). A rapid relative decline in the position of the United States occurs along with a rise in the role of Europe and Japan and the key role being played by producers of raw materials. This scenario differs radically from the trend-based scheme, insofar as in the first phase (1974-1980) the lessening of American influence makes way for the emergence of new blocs. This means:

- Europe is a political entity with a common European policy on transportation, aeronautical construction, industrialization, land planning, and social policies.

- Intrabloc trade rapidly develops and between neighboring blocs. International competition is lively, with export vital to countries without natural resources.

- Local conflicts persist, resulting from the rivalry between blocs, but the major prize becomes the conquest of the new El Dorado of the oceans.

- The supply of fossil fuels is no longer a constraint.

- The multinational firms are rarely multibloc firms.

- The international monetary system moves in the direction of the existence of several monetary zones - the yen zone, the European currency unit zone, the dollar zone. Floating exchange rates apply between these major currencies.

- The existence of homogeneous blocs facilitates an effective policy in dealing with the inflation problem.

Economic Position of France in the Context of a United Europe

The emergence of Europe as a political bloc leads to a high rate of economic growth (over 6% per annum), accompanied by the automation of industry. Socially there is general upward leveling reflected in 1) a reduction in the inequality of income distribution where it was greatest in Europe (France) and 2) a reduction in the work week in France and a tendency toward shorter holidays (a week in winter, a four-day week, or even three days for a minority).

Regional decentralization occurs for Europe as a whole. France becomes, from the point of view of population density, the desert of Europe, and the immigration of Europeans is substantial, but urbanization is planned, with a movement toward a mixed agricultural-urban society.

Improvements take place in the quality of life (rapid transport, housing, free time, more creative work, reduction in the retirement age).

The unification of Europe stirs popular opinion; a new system of values emerges. Income is no longer the only indicator of social success, and other factors such as free time and lifestyle become important. Along with money, knowledge becomes of key importance. Permanent education becomes a necessity and is facilitated by progress in telecommunications. Small differences in income are accompanied by larger and larger differences in lifestyle. The prestige of senior executives no longer results from their income, but rather from their freedom, and the free time they have in their work (working at home).

Consequences for Air Transport

1. Aeronautical construction

The European construction firms join together, giving them better control of the European market than in the past.

Europeans and Americans compete vigorously for the sale of aircraft to the other blocs, particularly the sale of military aircraft. The harmonization of European planning is accompanied by a diversification of aircraft types produced.

Within the context of a strong increase in traffic, the aeronautics firms (constructors) seek to maintain their technological lead. In particular they apply themselves to the construction of giant aircraft (800 seats, double-decker 747).

A trend toward the specialization of traffic (tourism, business, medium-haul, long-haul) leads the constructors to increase their range of diversification.

This competition does not preclude possible cooperation on certain projects, such as the construction of new engines, and the development of a super Concorde.

The balance of power is sufficiently favorable to Europe for the airbus to penetrate the American market, particularly since aircraft not meeting prescribed standards are phased out after 1978.

2. The airlines

European transport policy results in the creation of two pools of European airlines, one for serving the internal European market and the other for interbloc services. The internal European market presents the same characteristics as the internal American market, that is, 1) very heavy traffic, 2) low-fare structure to remain competitive with other forms of transport, and 3) specialist airlines (Air Inter and the third-level companies represent France in this internal pool).

The interbloc market, in which Air France together with the other European companies will engage, will show the same growth in the importance of long-haul routes as the North Atlantic, and similar vigorous competition will occur between the pools of airlines of the different blocs. The operating deficits of the long-haul routes will be made up by the strong increase in medium-haul traffice, which is more profitable.

3. Passenger traffic

Analysis at the national levels shows that in the period up to 1990, air transport will develop in a very favorable market because of:

- the reduction in inequality of income distribution.

- the high rate of economic growth.

- the increase in free time and the freer organization of work (working at home) for a substantial part of the population.

- increased migration.

- the lowering of fares.

- the reduction in retirement age.

These factors allow two typical passenger types to be described. The first
is a young employee of 25 to 30 years of age. He is not yet an executive but
already has the lifestyle of one, made possible because his wife goes to work.
The reduction in the work week allows him to enjoy a full family life with his
wife and two children. The couple takes one or two trips per year by charter,
with or without the children, which is possible insofar as the grandparents are
available (earlier retirement) and the tour operators make separate
arrangements for transport and for children's holidays.

The advent of this clientele, representing about 50% of the active
population, turns air transport into a form of mass transport.

The second is a senior executive whose weekly activity falls into two
categories: one part mobile (intensive travel) and the other part fixed (he
works at home). The work week is reduced to 3 or 4 days, of which one is
usually spent at home writing, catching up with information, etc. Telecommunications devices allow him to remain in contact with his firm. His second
home has become his main residence. Cheap annual season tickets allow him
to take the plane to go to his workplace which may be at a distance of more
than 300 miles from his home. This is an extension of the practice of airline
pilots, many of whom work in Paris and live on the Côte d'Azur. In spite of
progress in communications, he is frequently obliged to travel abroad for
professional reasons. Airports offer "burotels," which allow him to hold on-
the-spot meetings and to leave as quickly as possible afterwards.

Actors and Their Strategies

From Table 7-2, one can foresee certain conflicts and alliances.

First Conflict

A convergence of interest might link Paris Airport and the airlines, who
might be induced to exert pressure on the constructors to ensure that
projected new aircraft be more in line with the needs and constraints of the
traffic. This is the demand-supply conflict, which marks a certain
discontinuity with the past since supply has hitherto dominated demand. In
the future the airlines are destined to be much more closely associated with
the conception and exection of new projects.

Second Conflict

Paris Airport, supported this time by the constructors, may be induced to
put pressure on the airlines to purchase new aircraft that perform better in
terms of meeting certain pollution (noise) standards. This action may be
characterized by differential taxes and ban on night flights for certain types
of aircraft.

TABLE 7.2   Actors' Strategies in Air Transport System, 1983: Orientation SMIC [a]

Action on / of	CONSTRUCTORS	AIRLINES	STATE
CONSTRUCTORS	Objective To survive and avoid crisis Problems Plans for higher performance aircraft/specific noise and fuel consumption standards to meet Association between constructors Military orders Diversification of activities	Pressure on airlines to purchase new aircraft Diversification of needs and of aircraft Standardization of the fleet for each constructor Availability of entire range No significant technological progress	Exercise "blackmail" in regard to jobs Demand finance for new projects
AIRLINES	Demand aircraft better suited to their needs Dominant criterion: Cost per passenger mile or per ton effectively transported Reluctance to use large aircraft	Objective: To maintain market share Problems Financial Investment and salaries To maintain high frequency and occupancy Means Cooperation between airlines (ATLAS) Increased use of branches Standardization and operating flexibility of the fleet Development of freight Concentration at the tertiary level (feeder lines)	Seek protection from competition in the form of discriminatory rights in relation to long-haul traffic
STATE	To protect the national aeronautical industry Military and civil aircraft orders Finance for new projects Export credits Approaches to foreign governments Appeal to private finance	Protectionism Pressure on airlines to purchase Mercury Airbus with financial aid State protects airlines provided they develop and improve their section	Purpose Prestige and a French presence in the world Problems Unemployment Inflation Means Sustained growth

(a) Actors' analysis may be approached by means of a strategic table, of which the above forms an incomplete part only.

Third Conflict

The policy of diversification practiced by the Airport may be slowed down by the national airlines insofar as this dynamic approach would conflict with their main objectives: that their market share should not diminish too rapidly.

Fourth Conflict

There would be conflict between residents living near the airports, who wish to protect their environment, and Paris Airport, which requires space to exist and develop. The airport already practices a voluntary policy in this regard (indemnities, taxes, pressures on constructors and airlines). See the first and second conflicts. But if the pressure by the residents persists and intensifies, other concessions may have to be made. The residents in fact pose certain questions that require answers. Without necessarily going so far as to demand a ban on night flights, they wonder, for example, why cargo aircraft are not subjected to a tax on noise when many of them fly at night.

SITUATION IN 1983

We are interested in the situation of the actors in air transport in 1983. A certain number of potential conflicts have been brought to light from the table of actors' strategies. These conflicts translate into a certain number of linkages, which can be characterized by five "events." Further it is necessary to take into account another event external to the air transport system, which reflects changes in the balance of world forces.

List of Events Characterizing the 1983 Situation

e_1 Changes in balance of power toward a world of 5 blocs

This trend of events is important for the development of air transport. It is one of the key points that allow the trend-based and contrast scenarios to be sketched.

e_2 Creation of a European airline

This could be merely a reinforcement of links already existing between the airlines of the Atlas group.

e_3 The Airbus penetrates the domestic American market

The occurrence of this event would mean that the balance of power is sufficiently favorable to the European constructors to penetrate the American market and for the accent to be placed on economical and silent aircraft.

e_4 Aircraft not conforming to the 707 and DC8 standards forbidden to fly
into Europe, remodelled from 1978 on

Nearby residents would have been sufficiently active to oblige the airlines
to update their fleets and to permit the consructors to launch new aircraft in
greater conformity with noise standards.

e_5 Event "X" (confidential)

e_6 A giant French or foreign charter tour operator dominates the airlines

If a tour operator were to control a sufficiently large part of the market,
he would be able to lay down conditions to the airlines and to influence their
policy as to frequency of flights and character of fleets.

The Raw Data

The raw data for this situation are shown in Table 7-3.

TABLE 7.3 Events characterizing the 1983 situation

Probability

H_1 (a)	H_2 (b)			
0.6	0.2	e_1	=	change in the balance of power toward a world of five blocs
0.7	0.7	e_2	=	creation of a European airline
0.4	0.6	e_3	=	the airbus penetrates the domestic American market
0.6	0.7	e_4	=	aircraft outside the 707, DC8 standards forbidden to fly into Europe or replaced from 1978
0.4	0.3	e_5	=	event "X"
0.3	0.4	e_6	=	a French or other equivalent "Neckerman" (large German charter operator) dominates the airlines

(a) In H_1 we are relatively close to a world of five blocs.

(b) In H_2 the world remains in two blocs.

First, the group of experts consulted for this study made an independent
estimate of each conditional probability, without taking into account the
previous question. This avoids a bias that could arise from the order in which
the questions are asked.   Finally, the group estimated the individual

probabilities.   The two hypotheses adopted, H_1 and H_2, differ essentially in regard to the probability of e_1, as is seen in Table 7-3. This raw information is inconsistent in the sense that the classical axioms of probability are not obeyed. SMIC not only allows "net" results to be obtained (i.e., corrected and made consistent), but also gives us the probabilities of the scenarios.

The Results

For convenience, we shall first present and comment on the corrected results for the individual and conditional probabilities, according to the two hypotheses H_1 and H_2, and we shall then comment on the secenario probabilities that allowed the base information to be modified.

Comments

Individual Probabilities

For both H_1 and H_2, the individual probability of e_1 rises. This movement is particularly noticeable for H_2, where $P(e_1)$ moves from 0.20 to 0.32, indicating that the probability of reaching a world of five blocs is greater than was originally thought. The converse phenomenon can be noted for e_2. As $P(e_2)$ reduces from 0.7 to 0.64 and 0.60 (under hypotheses H_1 and H_2 respectively), the probability of the existence of a European airline in 1983 becomes smaller than expected. Further study of the results shows that there is a chance of 1 in 2 that the airbus will penetrate the domestic American market. Finally the probability of the existence of a powerful tour operator remains in the neighborhood of 0.4.

Conditional Probabilities

The changes in conditional probability are much larger, particularly under hypothesis H_2. This is explained by the fact that it is relatively contrasted in relation to the table of conditional probabilities. In fact, among the group of experts who filled out the table, a majority were in favor of H_1, and in consequence we shall pay particular attention to this hypothesis. Furthermore certain changes are particularly interesting since the probablities concerned become 0 or, at the other extreme, equal to 1.

On the basis of H_1 and H_2,

$P(2/5)$ increases from 0.8 to 1. If this event "X" occurs between now and 1983 it is certain that there will also be a European airline at that date.

On the basis of H_1,

$P(5/\bar{2})$ reduces from 0.2 to 0. In the context of a world of five blocs, if there is no European airline it is certain that event "C" will not occur.

On the basis of H_2,

on the other hand, $P(5/\bar{2})$ increases from 0.2 to 0.38. In the context of a world of 2 blocs, even without a European airline, the probability that "X" occurs is not negligible. Two more examples of large changes can be mentioned: $P(6/1)$ reduces from 0.8 to 0.45 under H_1 and H_2. The group of experts had overestimated the probability of having a powerful tour operator in the context of a world of five blocs. On the other hand the group had underestimated $P(2/\bar{1})$, i.e., the probability of having a European airline, given that there is no European policy, this figure increasing from 0.2 to about 0.4.

Scenario Probabilities

For 6 events there are $2^6 = 64$ possible states. With each state E_k is associated a probablitity π_k with $\Sigma\pi_k = 1$, since it is certain that one of these scenarios will in fact occur. The class of realizable scenarios (i.e., those having a nonzero probability) is more restricted for H_2 than for H_1 (17 realizable against 20). This means that under both hypotheses H_1 and H_2, among the 64 possible scenarios, 44 and 47 respectively have zero probabilities.

On the basis of H_1 and H_2 can be mentioned the example ES (110111) with $\pi 5 = 0$.

There is certainty that the airbus will penetrate the domestic American market if the five other events occur.

- E29 (110001) with $\pi 29 = 0$.   - E30 (010001) with $\pi 30 = 0$.

Whether or not there is a trend toward a world of five blocs, if the airbus does not penetrate the American market, or if aircraft below standard are not forbidden, and event "X" does not occur, it is certain that there will not be both a European airline and a powerful tour operator.

Trend Group of Scenarios

On the basis of H_1, there is more than 1 chance in 2 that one of the five scenarios E33, E32, E17, E45, E38 will correspond to the situation in 1983.

The most likely of these is E33 (111110) with $\pi 33 = 0.151$. This is the scenario of the strong Europe: the tour operators have not managed to associate themselves in the face of a powerful European airline, event "X" occurs, aircraft not meeting standards are forbidden, and the airbus penetrates the domestic American market.

We then have scenario E32 (000001), which is the scenario of a weak Europe complementary in every way to the foregoing scenario. On the basis of H_2, there is more than 1 chance in 2 that one of the four following scenarios, E32, E17, E38, E52, will correspond to the 1983 situation. The most likely of these is E32 with $\pi 32$ equal to 0.198. This is the scenario of a weak Europe. This result, already mentioned, is quite logical within the context of a world of two blocs.

It should be noticed that this scenario corresponds to the occurrence of one event to the exclusion of all the others. This is event e_6, however, which has a relatively modest probability, 0.4; almost half of this probability, however, is concentrated in state E32.

E17 and E38 belong to the two groups of trend-based scenarios under both H_1 and H_2.

Also in this group is E52 (001100) with $\pi 52$ equal 0.113. This provides for a world of two blocs without a united Europe, without a European airline, aircraft not meeting the standards being forbidden because of noise, and the airbus being well placed to penetrate the domestic American market.

Contrasted Scenarios

Certain very unlikely scenarios can be described as contrasted. Under hypothesis H_1 can be mentioned: E21 (110101) with $\pi 21 = 0.022$.

It is unlikely that the airbus will not penetrate the domestic American market and that event "X" will not occur if there is a European airline and if aircraft not meeting standards are forbidden and if the tour operators are powerful.

Under Hypothesis H_2 can be mentioned: E54 (010100) with $\pi 54 = 0.031$.

It is unlikely that the airbus will not penetrate the domestic American market and that event "X" will not happen when there is a European airline, and when aircraft not meeting standards are forbidden.

Sensitivity Analysis

The sensitivity analysis consists of studying the variation ΔP_J in P_J following a variation ΔP_i in P_i: We calculate the elasticity

$$e_{iJ} = \frac{\Delta P_J}{P_J} \ / \ \frac{\Delta P_i}{P_i}$$

The creation of a European airline and the existence of a powerful tour operator are <u>motor events</u> for the development of air transport.

It can be seen that the phenomenon of a politically united Europe does not have a very strong impact on a system:

$$\sum_J |e_{1J}| = 1.13$$

Study of the column totals shows that certain <u>events</u> are more <u>dominated</u> than others under e_5 with

$$\sum_i |e_{i5}| = 3.91 \quad \text{and} \ e_6 \ \text{with} \ \sum_i |e_{i6}| = 3.69$$

In relation to e_5 the result is mainly explained by $e_{2J} = 2.05$, signifying that if the probability of e_2 increases by 100%, that of e_5 increases by 200%. The occurrence of "X" is strongly conditioned by the creation of a European airline.

Event e_6 is both a dominated and a motor event. The power of the tour operators is therefore the most sensitive event from the point of view of the development of the air transport system.

The particular case of $e_{46} = -1.25$ is of interest; if the probability of e_4 increases by 100%, that of e_6 decreases by 125%. The banning of aircraft not meeting standards is therefore an event unfavorable to tour operators and delays the arrival of an equivalent to "Neckerman" (a major German charter tour operator) in France.

8 Retrospective and Prospective Study of Energy: A Reading of the Crisis

We present a retrospective and prospective reading of the energy "crisis" drawn from studies recently carried out at SEMA Prospective. This chapter comprises three parts.

The retrospective part recalls that this is not the first energy "crisis" the Western world has experienced and shows the extent to which the behavior of the actors explains past developments.

The analysis of the present situation allows the plans of the main actors - Western countries, Organization of Petroleum-Exporting Countries (OPEC) - to be identified and tomorrow's conflicts to be foreseen.

The prospective part shows how the SMIC method allows the most likely energy scenarios up to the year 1990 to be determined.

RETROSPECTIVE STUDY SINCE THE 1920s

Recent upheavals in the world oil situation have brought energy to the forefront of current affairs. Energy sources competing with OPEC oil (uranium, off-shore, etc.) are regarded by many experts as likely to replace it just as it replaced coal. Are structural changes involved, or is too much weight being attached in current thinking to a crisis that is merely conjunctural? Who are the decisive actors in the world energy system? What were and are their strategies? Answers must be made to each of these questions.

The year 1973 did not see the first energy "crisis" the Western world has known. We need only to look at the situations in the years 1928 and 1956.

The 1928 Crisis

In 1928 the fear of shortages conjured up prospects of a difficult future in which it might be necessary to resort to oil substitutes such as alcohol and shale (see Note 1). At that time world reserves were variously estimated for

93

15-50 years consumption. In 1924 a "congress for studying the transformation
of domestic raw mineral and vegetable materials into fuels capable of
replacing oil derivatives" was held in Paris. In 1930 in Berlin the problem of
energy imports arose, and it is remarkable that solutions proposed at the
time, apart from those processes that were not meant very seriously, are
similar to those mentioned today: manufacture of synthetic oil by distillation
of bituminous shale, the hydrogenation of pit coal, and the carbonization of
lignites.

The vital and unforeseeable factor was the size of deposits in the Middle
East (60% of today's world reserves). These discoveries banished fears of an
energy shortage until 1956.

In 1928 a prospective reading of the fundamental aspects of energy
problems included an analysis of the relationship between the British and
French decline on the one hand and the economic expansion of American
economic power on the other. It was then that an agreement was reached
between the future major producers, whose doctrine was to achieve
agreement on production, so as to stabilize the price of crude, and limited
competition on the market. The year 1928 was marked by a number of events
of great importance for oil that passed completely unnoticed.

The 1956 Crisis

The year 1956 is a second key period for the study of contemporary energy
problems. It was a year of political crisis, and the closing of the Suez Canal
was to be important both in its energy repercussions and because it brought
about the eclipse of France and Great Britain as international powers.

The problem of energy supply was seen at that time in relation to an
economic growth that no one believed could continue for twenty years
unchecked. A misanalysis of the 1956 situation resulted in a shortage of oil,
the introduction of nuclear energy, a comeback for coal - and forecasts that
appear erroneous today both in order of magnitude and in terms of the
structure of energy anticipated for the period 1970-1975.

In parallel with this, the notion of the security of energy supply was
developed following the Suez affair. This led governments to diversify
geographically their sources of production (in particular Africa) and to
provide (particularly in Europe) research budgets for nuclear energy. In 1957
EURATOM was created. However, these ambitious programs were not
realized, either for coal (see Note 2) or for nuclear energy, as is shown by the
British example. In 1957 the nuclear program was tripled, and it was
expected that by 1970 nuclear energy would provide 40% of British
electricity. But in the next three years, and even before orders for
generating stations had been made, the program was reduced by one half.
Today nuclear energy represents only 10% of the electricity production. The
British nuclear industry never recovered.

These forecasting errors are partly explained by the profound transformations in the oil market at the time. Middle East crude, repelled from the
American market as a result of the introduction of import quotas by
President Eisenhower in 1958 for reasons of domestic policy, was diverted
massively towards Europe. The quota regulations limited the quantities of oil

imports in relation to the refining capacity in the United States. Thus the independents, who produced oil in the Middle East and had no refining capacity, saw the American market close up completely. Coal, like nuclear energy, was unable to stand up to the dumping carried out particularly by independent American companies, which sold in Europe the oil that could not be imported into the United States.

Simultaneously, other factors brought downward pressure to bear on oil prices: productivity improvements, technical progress, economies of scale (increases in refinery and tanker size).

Once the crisis had passed, the price of nuclear electricity appeared less and less competitive in particular because of the increases in interest rates brought about by an already high rate of inflation) compared with oil, which was becoming more and more abundant and cheap. (In the 1960s the real price of oil was continuously falling.) Similarly natural gas, whose cleanness made it attractive, saw its development impeded by the low price of competing oil. The 1956 crisis resulted in the prosperity of the uranium industries until 1959, a year in which 33,000 tons of uranium were mined, at a turnover of some $1000 million at an average price for uranium of $16 a pound.

But in 1959, in the context of cheap oil, the United States did not renew its contracts for the supply of uranium. As a result, production declined - the United States alone represented over half of the demand - to a level of hardly 15,000 tons in 1966 and a price varying between $4 and $5 a pound. This state of crisis resulted in the closing of many uranium-producing factories (about 50) and the underutilization ($\pm$70%) of others. The ambitious nuclear program of the end of the 1950s was not translated into fact.

Behavior of the Actors 1965 to 1973

The oil-exporting countries, the oil multinationals, and governments comprised the main actors in the oil system of this period.

a) The increasing role of the oil-exporting countries.

The creation of OPEC in 1960 should have attracted more attention, because the events that occurred later in the oil world between 1965 and 1973 had their origins in that event.

● the demand that production be controlled by the countries of origin and that at least parts of the crude oil produced be refined locally,

● the Teheran agreement of 14 February concluded between the OPEC countries and the oil companies, following the offensive initiated by Algeria, Libya, and Iraq, which revised crude prices upwards,

● the nationalization (to the extent of 51%) of French oil companies active in Algeria,

● the increasing awareness of the exporting countries of their solidarity,

- their ability to act collectively toward the consumer countries, and the necessity to act very rapidly, since over the long term the strategic position of oil producers would decline.

b) The new strategies of the oil companies

The relative fall in oil prices determined by the oil companies allowed the majors to get rid of the independents whose margins could not survive the drop in crude prices and led to an unprecedented expansion in oil consumption at the expense of the competing fuels (coal, nuclear energy).

Faced, however, with the predicted exhaustion of oil at the beginning of the next century, the oil companies have not limited their strategy to the maintenance of their control over oil, but are aiming also to extend their influence into other fields to control future energy resources. This desire is reflected in their tendency to take stakes in the coal and nuclear industries.

The oil companies, strongly established in the nuclear energy industry, sought to upgrade their investments, which had hitherto been unprofitable in this area because of the many technical difficulties encountered, and particularly, the powerful resistance of ecological groups to the establishment of nuclear power stations.

It was with this intention that the oil companies in the summer of 1973 staged an artificial shortage of gasoline in the United States in order to put pressure on the American administration and to reduce the opposition to nuclear developments. These same oil companies were, like OPEC, in favor of a heavy increase in crude prices on the world market, which would:

- make the exploitation of American coal and nuclear energy immediately profitable.

- considerably increase their production profits, in spite, paradoxically, of a very large increase in the taxation of the host countries.

c) The American government's new strategy toward the rise of Europe and Japan

Since 1950 the United States has undergone a relative economic decline, (see Table below) which is reflected particularly in the deficit in their balance of payments, the devaluation of the dollar, and the abandonment of the gold-exchange standard.

TABLE 8.1 Share of U.S.A. in GDP of OECD Countries[a]

	1950 %	1960 %	1970 %	1980 %
USA	61.0	54.6	48.2	40
OECD	100	100	100	100

(a) Precrisis forecast from a study by GEPI

After 1965-1966, the United States government realized that the rate of growth of the proven reserves of American petroleum was historically at its lowest level ever (see Note 3).

At the same time, cheap oil was being massively imported, and American energy dependence was on the increase, although never to the same degree as that of European countries because United States dependence was mainly on nearby countries such as Canada or Venezuela.

Furthermore, exploration for new oil deposits in the United States continued to diminish, and the reserves expressed in terms of years based on current consumption levels fell drastically. Imports of oil products continued to represent an increasing part of the national consumption, in spite of a fleeting recovery in 1967 and 1968.

The United States was thus confronted with a double threat, both on the energy and political levels. The American government believed first of all that the reestablishment of its domination of Europe and Japan could be achieved through an alliance with the Soviet Union and the socialist bloc. This is the significance of the agreements of economic cooperation signed with the socialist countries and of the policy of peaceful co-existence.

Since 1965, the construction of nuclear power stations was resumed, thus opening up new outlets for uranium, but the demand was not enough in relation to the level of supply to provide much impetus to the market, and uranium prices remained low: $6 per pound at the end of 1972. Such levels did not encourage exploration, particularly since reserves remained large. This explains why at the beginning of the 1970s, uranium had been discovered in only 10% of the regions in the world that were geologically likely to contain it. Prospecting was carried out only where this could be achieved at very low cost. The map of world uranium reserves in 1972 was as developed as that for oil in 1928.

The setback to the hesitant upswing in American nuclear activity at the end of the 1960s cannot be explained merely in terms of the technical difficulties encountered (almost one power station out of every two did not work), but also by the rise of the ecological movement.

American energy dependence continued to grow. In 1972 the United States was, together with Japan, the largest world importer of oil products.

The Crisis of 1973 to 1975

The tendency for oil prices to decline as a result of the policies of the major oil companies contains the seeds of the following countertendencies:

1. Massive imports of oil products represented an increasingly large proportion of total American oil consumption (6% in 1955 and 55% in 1973). Forecasts showed that this dependence was likely to rise, with

domestic production hardly increasing or even falling off in the years 1971 to 1973. The security of supplies was in question. The United States government could not ignore this.

2. The relative economic decline of the United States was becoming more and more pronounced (1971). It was underlined by the unfavorable balance of payments and the devaluation of the dollar.

3. The reserves of hydrocarbon fuels are not unlimited, and preparations had to be made for the post-petroleum era (see Note 4), since the major companies wished to show a return on the investments made in nuclear energy.

4. The rise of OPEC was making itself felt and was to be as inexorable as the process of decolonization. It would therefore be necessary to accept with good grace an increase in oil prices that was actually only making up for earlier shortfalls (see Note 5).

In April 1973 President Nixon abolished import quotas for oil and replaced them with a flexible system of taxes, which allowed the American government to regulate oil imports according to the energy policy of the United States.

During the summer of 1973, i.e., before the Arab-Israeli October war, the American oil companies organized an artificial shortage of gasoline in the United States itself, particularly in the regions where the nuclear challenge was strongest. The supply in Europe at the same time was quite normal (see Note 6). From October 1973 the price rises, which are so familiar, began to occur. At the same time:

● the nuclear energy field, in which American oil companies dominated, became competitive,

● explorations for oil in the United States showed unprecedented increases, in spite of ever-higher drilling costs,

● by virtue of their dependence on oil, the economic and political rise of the European countries and of Japan was slowed, thus offsetting the relative American decline,

● the exploitation of off-shore deposits was accelerated,

● oil company profits have never been higher than in 1973,

● the "energy crisis" served as an alibi for the crisis in the Western economic system, which may have had other causes (inflation, etc).

Finally, what happened in 1928, 1956, 1973 in an area as strategic as energy, results from changes in the world balance of power and from the confrontation between the plans of the oil companies and of the producing and consuming countries. These key dates have had important repercussions. It is therefore suitable to link energy prospects to changes in the balance of power between the actors in the energy system.

The year 1973 marked the ending of past trends and the emergence of countertrends (new balance of power, relatively expensive energy, development of energy sources competing with oil, etc.). This break is all the more significant at present, since the Western world is wrestling with its greatest economic and political crisis since the second World War. Will counter-trends arise? This is the question to be answered in the prospective section. The analysis of the present situation, however, already provides some elements of an answer.

PRESENT SITUATION AND ACTORS' PLANS

The analysis of the current situation - the years 1973-1975 - consists of examining the plans of the actors. The next stage is to specify in the light of these strategies to what extent the events that have happened since 1973 can confirm or invalidate the implementation of one or another plan.

As has already been emphasized in the retrospective part, energy history is closely related to that of oil. We have noted in particular that the failure of energy programs launched after the Suez crisis is explained by the relative drop in oil prices imposed by the oil companies.

The recurrence of such a situation appears to be excluded. High oil prices, in fact, accord well with the fundamental strategy of the oil companies and, to a lesser extent, of the Western countries. It is the sine qua non for a profitable exploitation of off-shore deposits, for the competitiveness of nuclear energy, and for greater energy self-sufficiency.

Nevertheless, as will be shown, this does not mean that the OPEC countries will necessarily be able to sell all their oil at this price.

As in 1928, 1956, and 1973, what happens between now and 1990 in the field of energy will result from changes in the balance of world power, and in particular from the relative weight of the United States.

In order to examine the strategy of the actors involved, we shall basically draw on the conclusions of recent studies in which their respective plans show up quite clearly:

- in the case of the Western countries, one study carried out by OECD (see Note 7) and the other by GEPI (See Note 8).

- for OPEC countries, the different memoranda presented by Algeria to the United Nations and to OPEC (see Note 9).

We shall speak of the OPEC plan and the Western plan. It will of course be realized that the reference to a plan common to several countries does not exclude the existence of internal divergences among these countries, but simply means that at a given moment in world development, the convergence of interests (or domination) between certain actors has allowed this or that alliance to happen. The fulfillment of these plans of course depends on the maintenance of some cohesion, and supposes that internal contradictions will not develop to such an extent as to break up the alliance.

The Western Project

Price Hypotheses: An Important Contradiction

In the two studies already mentioned, several hypotheses regarding oil prices are made. (The "independence" plan will not be referred to, since it is only "the detailed American part of the OECD Report" and contains the same hypotheses about petroleum prices.)

TABLE 8.2 Price per Barrel in January 1, 1974 dollars

	OECD	GEPI
Low hypothesis	$3	$6
Medium hypothesis	$6	$7.5
High hypothesis	$9	$9

These studies show that "even on the $9 hypothesis, oil imports will continue to increase between now and 1980." In fact, in each case "oil in 1990 will meet approximately 50% of primary energy needs of the OECD countries; nuclear energy only 10%" (see Note 10).

However, it is not certain that the OPEC countries will be able to sell all their oil at this high price. The pressure on the price of oil, particularly in those exporting countries that are densely populated and have high foreign-exchange requirements (Algeria, Iran), will be all the stronger for the fact that "the demand by Western countries might be 20% less than that expected before the crisis" (see Note 11). Furthermore a drop in oil prices would ease the foreign exchange burden of the European countries and Japan. This is what the GEPI study in fact envisages.

"The solidarity between producers could be broken in the event of a low rate of growth of purchases by industrial countries or the discovery of large new deposits; there might even be serious conflicts of a political nature between OPEC members" (see Note 12).

This hypothesis also appears in the OECD study and is expressed through two apparently contradictory propositions: 1) High-priced oil is the sine qua non for the viable development of offshore oil and nuclear energy. 2) The development of offshore oil and nuclear energy is the necessary condition for the drop in oil prices.

It is legitimate to study the meaning of this contradiction. There are two possibilities: either this contradiction is more apparent than real, or else it will tend to grow in importance and create a new situation.

1. Apparent contradiction: settlement of oil prices at medium level

The contradiction is only apparent and oil prices settle at a medium level, sufficiently high not to threaten the competitiveness of nuclear energy. Meanwhile the exploitation of offshore oil remains low as a result of increasing supplies of oil in the face of stable demand.

2. Real contradiction and "two-tier market" in energy

A reinforcement of this contradiction can be imagined, finding expression, for example, in the creation of a two-tier market in energy, a high price for the production of OECD energy and a low price for purchase of non-OECD oil. This prospect is envisaged in the OECD report, which says, "Oil from the OECD zone is expensive in comparison with oil from the OPEC countries, and the question arises how domestic production could be protected against possible cheap imports (see Note 13).

The American Scenario: "A Two-Tier Market for Energy"

There is already a precedent for the thesis of a two-tier market, as the GEPI study points out. "In the decade 1960-1970 the American government attempted to disconnect its internal market from the world market almost completely" (see Note 14).

Thus, under the pretext of providing for the survival of the small local producers, the quota law allowed the large American oil companies to make windfall gains. In fact as already described in the retrospective part and confirmed by experts during the 1960s, the large oil companies made massive imports of oil at lower and lower prices to sell on a protected national market. Thus, on the basis of this hypothesis, the OECD countries would be as protected in energy as Europe is today in the field of agriculture. The OECD countries would thus reap the double benefit of reducing their energy dependence on the OPEC countries by developing indigenous resources (nuclear energy, offshore oil, coal) and by exercising pressure on the demand for non-OECD-produced energy so as to get it for the lowest possible price. It should not be forgotten, however, that the OECD study reflects predominantly the American position. In this regard it should be noticed that the most favorable hypothesis for the United States (one in which, according to the GEPI study, the price of energy is low - $6) also corresponds to the medium hypothesis (the most desirable?) in the OECD study.

TABLE 8.3 The four "scenarios" in the GEPI Study

	Price of Energy	Effort at self-sufficiency
Scenario 1	Low $6	Intense
Scenario 2	Medium $7.5	Intense
Scenario 3	Medium $7.5	Moderate
Scenario 4	High $9	Moderate

Scenario 1: the strategy of the "two-tier market in energy"

This is the most favorable scenario for the United States. The cumulative surplus of its current operations amounts to $87.7 billion (1974 prices) (see Note 15). This surplus more than compensates for the external deficits of the other countries. The financial balance of the OECD zone can therefore be assured as long as the United States and the United Kingdom help Europe and Japan.

In many ways this scenario is very close to the two-tier market described previously. It is based on an intense effort toward self-sufficiency in energy (offshore deposits, nuclear energy, coal), necessarily at great cost, and with an energy price which corresponds to the minimum price demanded by the United States; at a price lower than this the two-tier system would be too dificult to impose on Europe and on Japan. This means of course that some energy is imported from outside OECD. This scenario calls for a coalition between rich developed but energy-poor countries directed by the United States to its great advantage. In this situation:

- The development of offshore oil and nuclear energy are profitable,

- The OPEC countries can expect their receipts to diminish, slowing down the industrial advances of the Third World,

- Europe and Japan remain dependent on the United States: economically in regard to the supply of oil and enriched uranium, and financially since American aid is required to make up the external deficit of the other OECD countries.

- The relative decline of the United States is halted.

- The world remains divided between the United States and the Soviet Union, two blocs.

Scenarios Nos. 2 and 3: moderate energy prices

In these two scenarios, the United States would not have succeeded in imposing a two-tier price system for energy, and energy prices would settle at a moderate level.

Scenario No. 2 would be almost as favorable for the United States as the preceding one, since the cumulative surplus of American operations would amount to $86 billion in constant 1974 prices ($87.7 billion in No. 1). On the other hand, with European and Japanese deficits much higher and the American surplus insufficient to cover them, the OECD as a whole would go into deficit. The effort toward self-sufficiency would remain intense, particularly on the part of the Americans. Europe and Japan would diversify their energy sources but continue to import large quantities of hydrocarbon fuel from the OPEC countries. In this scenario, Europe and Japan would achieve greater independence from the OPEC countries, but at the price of becoming more dependent on the United States.

In scenario 3 the effort to become self-sufficient on the part of the OECD countries is more moderate, and the over-all OECD deficit represents five times the American surplus. This scenario is much less favorable for the United States than the preceding ones, since the total surplus of their operations between 1974 and 1980 represents only 40% of that in scenarios 1 and 2. Europe and Japan would hardly rely on the United States any more, but would seek to conclude agreements directly with the OPEC countries. The relative decline of the Western countries would appear more pronounced in relation to the industrial rise of the Third World. New blocs would emerge; the world of two blocs would be no more.

Scenario No. 4

From the Western point of view, this is the pessimistic scenario. Energy prices would be high and the effort toward self-sufficiency would be moderate in its results. The OECD countries as a whole would experience a considerable trade deficit, which could be eliminated only through a slowing down of economic activity.

Conclusion: The Western Plan Does Not Envisage a High Energy Price

It is worth noting the absence of a fifth scenario, with high energy prices and an intense effort toward self-sufficiency - the high price justifying the effort, and the prospect of self-sufficiency the high price. The OECD countries hardly consider the hypothesis of a high price. In other words, they do not believe that during the period 1975-1990 they will have to purchase OPEC oil as expensively as in 1974.

The OPEC Plan

This plan assumes strong cohesion between the different members of OPEC. It is directed toward establishing a new economic world order, allowing the developing countries to become fully integrated as actors in the world economic system. This integration requires that the terms of trade should be redefined along the following lines:

- The progressive loss of purchasing power of the currency is controlled, or at least effectively reduced. To do this, the developing countries demand to share effective power within the international financial organizations - International Monetary Fund (IMF), and World Bank (IBRD).

- Oil must be available on terms that permit both the resumption of growth by the industrialized countries (which is necessary to the developing countries) as well as the development of the developing countries.

- This can be achieved only through a transfer of technology between the industrialized and the developing countries, which is essential to allow the developing countries to balance their foreign trade accounts after the 1980s.

By that time world requirements for oil will be relatively lower (because of competition from new sources of energy, particularly nuclear energy and gas), and the OPEC share of this production will be in decline (because of off-shore developments in the United States, Arctic, USSR, China). Furthermore, internal consumption in the OPEC countries will have increased considerably by virtue of their development. This will contribute in an important measure to the reduction of the quantities available for export. At the same time imports of goods and services will be rising, leading eventually to a deficit in their balance of payments.

At the conference of heads of state of the OPEC countries, Algeria presented a memorandum arguing for an oil price policy along the following lines:

- Between 1975 and 1980 the price (in real terms) should be frozen, thus allowing the industrialized countries to right their economies hit by inflation and to a lesser extent by rises in energy costs. (This price freeze of crude would also slow the substitution of other energy sources.)

- After 1980, oil prices would be raised to the mean level of all energy prices. They would be indexed partly to the prices of capital and consumer goods imported by the developing countries and partly to an indicator, still to be defined, representing the cost of development for the developing countries. (The rates of inflation for these products have been 3-4 points higher than the rates of inflation in the industrialized countries, which were used for the basis of the indexing calculations.)

Thus, the inclusion of the costs of development, together with a periodic readjustment of prices, should allow the OPEC countries to redress their balance of payments and to continue to create the economic apparatus vital to their long-term survival (see Note 16).

The technological development of the developing countries also calls for new juridical structures. Current legislation concerning, for example, clauses in "turnkey" contracts, the granting of patent rights, or arbitration procedures in the case of disputes, too often favors the industrialized countries. What is therefore required is the definition of new procedures guaranteeing that what the customer is buying is in accordance with the seller's specifications. These procedures should be based on the principle of giving the seller of technology a stake in the actual results (see Note 17), and on warranties provided by the industrialized countries.

The plan also aims at allowing its members a determining role in the world political arena, particularly in contributing to the development of the Third World. In 1974 more than 10% of the GNP of the OPEC countries was devoted to Third World credits. The creation of a fund for development of international cooperation (FDIC) is envisaged, whose purpose would be less to assure the financial power of OPEC, than to lessen the financial hegemony of certain countries in providing resources to the Third World. It also envisages the promotion of nitrate fertilizer production in order to realize the agricultural potential of the developing countries. Further, in order to

protect Third World production, substantial stocks of raw materials and
agricultural products would be established to control price movements in
these products.

To summarize, the objective of the plan is to assure the development of
member countries through new terms of trade, making possible real transfers
of technology, to control the international monetary system by strengthening
the voice of member countries in the decision-making of the large world
organizations, and by weakening the American hegemony over the financial
resources to which the Third World has access. It envisages increasing
control over markets in industrial and agricultural raw materials, and a world
political role for OPEC in support of the Third World. This plan is built on
the expectation of solidarity of OPEC and on effective cooperation by the
industrialized countries.

Recent Developments

The era of cheap and plentiful energy is finally over. Western countries
will long continue to be dependent on OPEC oil. Comparing the 1974 and
1976 OECD projections of imports, it is seen that, despite a downward
revision of total energy needs of about 7% (5218 million tons oil equivalent
(TOE) instead of 5603 million TOE), oil imports will be considerably higher
than expected (1750 million TOE as against 1019). They will thus be double
the domestic production of the OECD zone (revised downward) rather than
three quarters.

While hitherto the main deficit zones have been Europe and Japan,
American oil dependence has increased sharply in recent months. In the first
half of 1977, American monthly oil imports were running at five times their
1973 level. As much as 39% of American consumption originated in OPEC
(particularly Venezuela), while national production is dropping 6% a year (see
Note 18). The United States is a long way from its objectives of energy
independence. Will the Carter plan be consigned to oblivion? It is not
impossible. The reason for this colossal forecasting error is found in the costs
of oil substitutes (nuclear energy and other new energies), which are proving
much less competitive than was thought in 1974 (see Note 19).

Thus, despite the quadrupling of oil prices since 1973, they remain
relatively low ($12 per barrel), since bringing them into line with the costs of
substitutes would, according to some estimates, lead to a further doubling. It
can therefore be expected that energy prices will be bid substantially upward,
particularly with certain - alarmist? - reports forecasting shortages in 1983-
85. World coal reserves, however, are probably five or six times higher than
those of oil. Substantial development of coal production will be possible,
notably in North America and the USSR. The coal will either be burned
directly, or transformed into gas or synthetic oil. In any case, pollution
problems will arise, and it is not clear whether consumers will be prepared to
accept the disadvantages associated with a massive return to coal. Coal
reserves are estimated to be sufficient to support a substantial rise in
consumption, but the largest reserves are to be found in the Middle East, thus
remote from the centers of consumption. Transport is much more costly in

large quantities and over long distances than for oil.

The most uncertain field is nuclear energy. Most nuclear programs are currently either behind schedule or being slowed down. In the United States, where President Carter has just drafted a huge energy program, the development of fast breeder reactors has been shelved, together with plans for reprocessing and recycling spent nuclear fuel. In Sweden, a public opinion unfavorable toward a substantial nuclear program has contributed to the unseating of a government. In Great Britain, where nuclear generators have long contributed to the grid, further development is almost nil. In fact, France is one of the few countries with a substantial program. It is thus still unclear what role nuclear energy will play in the year 2000. Furthermore, it is considered that the share of hydroelectric power will remain roughly constant at 5% of world energy needs, and the so-called "new" energies (solar, geothermal, "green" energy, etc.) will contribute little, in view of the present level of technology, to replacing oil after 1990.

While waiting for new moves leading to a doubling or tripling of oil prices, the large oil companies pursue a strategy of over-all control of the energy sector. Their power was somewhat challenged when OPEC took control of their activities, leading them to develop strategies of further geographical and technological diversification. Acting on public opinion to bring about an awareness of the urgency of the problems, they hope to obtain a carte blanche from governments to take in hand our nuclear future.

In the United States, they are the object of regular attacks by a section of public opinion. Congress has pressed for their breakup and President Carter has accused them of turning to their own profit the measures and efforts of the American people to improve the energy situation (the Carter plan). But the American oil companies have representatives at all levels in the administration, and it is unlikely that their power is actually jeopardized.

The industrialized countries have discussed the problem at great length, but have not done much. Here lies the real danger of the world energy situation. It may become critical before corrective action is taken, as is shown by the abundance of speeches, compared with the slight progress made.

Conclusions

Several conclusions can be drawn from the foregoing. On the one hand, long-term prospects for the Third World and the industrialized countries under this perspective are not compatible without the latter's acceptance of a certain relative decline. On the other hand, there is no indication that the industrialized countries and in particular the United States are ready to accept such a decline. It may even be thought that they will do everything to prevent it from happening.

The Western and OPEC plans are in conflict in many ways, particularly in relation to energy prices after 1980. In this situation of latent conflict, power continues to determine energy prices, and not any balance between supply and demand.

What actually happens will of course depend on the evolution of the balance of power. In the view of the author, the United States will continue to play a determining role up to 1990. In other words, scenarios 1 and 2 remain possible. It is not certain, however, that Europe and Japan will rally to the American plan. Furthermore, a coalition between energy-poor industrialized countries and energy-rich underdeveloped countries might lead to the emergence of new blocs and bring about the relative decline of the United States.

Account must also be taken of the technological aspects (relative success or failure of nuclear energy, offshore exploration) of the new discoveries of oil. (Most of the experts the author has met feel that the actual resources are three times the official figures, but that this is concealed for strategic reasons.)

Finally, the role of the Soviet Union, which might supply the West with energy (and thus compete directly with OPEC oil) in exchange for American supplies of grain and Western assistance in the opening up of Siberia, should not be ignored.

ELEMENTS OF THE ENERGY PROSPECTIVE

The future is multiple, and several potential futures are possible. The path that leads to this or that future is not necessarily unique. The description of a potential future and the paths leading to it comprise a scenario. It is not possible here to describe the sequence of steps that make up the paths leading to the final results of each scenario.

Nevertheless, it is important to list the basic hypotheses that lead to the preliminary outlines of some of the final images of the future. It is the scenarios method which describes consistent paths leading from the present situation to the intermediate and final images. Such description, however, is beyond the scope of this exposition. In consequence we shall limit ourselves to the description of the fundamental geoenergy hypotheses that have gone into each of the scenarios.

The evolution of the international oil situation in the period 1975 to 1990 would be characterized by the occurrence or not of six fundamental hypotheses, suggested by the analysis of plans of the different actors concerned.

Examination of the probabilities of the occurrence of each hypothesis (simple and conditional probabilities) allows each expert to determine the scenarios he considers most likely to occur. A scenario is therefore represented by the interplay of six fundamental hypotheses, each of them either occurring or not occurring during the period.

A comparison of the different results leads to the emergence of several scenarios that the experts agree as the most likely. The reference scenario is the one considered, over all, to have the highest probability of occurrence. Associated with it are two contrasted scenarios, chosen from among the range of probable scenarios, so as to enrich the investigation by the study of possible divergent developments.

Fundamental Geoenergetic Hypotheses

The situations possible in 1990 are characterized by the occurrence or not (during the period 1975-1990) of the six following hypotheses:

H1. Maintenance of American leadership.

H2. OPEC solidarity.

H3. Maintenance of power by the major oil companies.

H4. Substantial increase in hydrocarbon reserves in the regions not controlled by OPEC.

H5. The fixing of a minimum oil price of about $7-8 per barrel.

H6. Strong increase in offshore activities.

Maintenance of American Leadership

The implication of this hypothesis is that in the year 1990 the world will be basically divided into two spheres of influence, by virtue of a de facto American-Soviet alliance.

In this situation, technological, military, financial, and economic domination of the United States over its sphere of influence will be maintained. Whether in OECD-US relations or Third World-US relations, it is American policy that sets the tone. In the field of energy, this is reflected in an OPEC-IEA (International Energy Agency) dialogue.

Europe, which has not established itself as a political entity, will have been unable to develop a common energy policy. (The North Sea is not European.) This does not preclude the promotion of an autonomous energy policy by certain "dissident" countries (France, for example).

Solidarity of Oil-Exporting Countries (OPEC)

This hypothesis implies a strengthening of OPEC - as opposed to a collapse - its expansion to include other oil-exporting countries and its extension to the whole range of hydrocarbon fuels (oil, gas).

Solidarity is sufficiently strong so that some countries accept the reduction of their exports to maintain energy prices at a level satisfactory for OPEC as a whole.

In spite of economic and political differences, OPEC countries present a united front on oil policy (although differences in manner of application may continue) and adopt a common line in the dialogue between rich and poor countries.

Maintenance of Power by the Major Oil Companies

The large multinational oil companies keep their control over the energy sector. In spite of loss of access to a part of the production, the oil multinationals keep their share of control of activities downstream (transport, refining, and particularly distribution), and upstream (research and exploration).

Their technological and commercial power is not diminished by the emergence of state-run companies in the producing countries, which do not manage to gain a sufficient foothold in the market for finished products.

The various lobbies hostile to the major oil companies do not become a major force. It will be remembered that in 1975, these movements were aimed at the dismemberment of the multinational companies (antitrust laws), at state intervention (state-run or federal American companies), and at barring the large oil companies from involvement in non-oil activities (nuclear energy, coal, etc.).

Substantial Increase in Hydrocarbon Reserves Outside OPEC Zone

The search for new oil zones (the Arctic, Greenland, USSR, China, etc.) reveals, not later than 1980, the existence of substantial resources, thereby fundamentally altering the present situation.

By the same token, the thesis that the size of Western resources may be more than three times the official figures proves to be correct.

(In our view a technological revolution would not have significant effect within our time frame, because of the inertia of the structures.)

Oil Price Minimum of $7-8 Per Barrel (1975 Dollars)

Rather than speculate on the possible price of oil, it is preferable to ask whether there will be sufficient profitability (floor price between $8 and $10 per barrel) to guarantee energy investments during the period 1975-1990.

Strong Increase in Offshore Activities

The mean annual rate of growth of world production of offshore oil during the period 1975-1990 would be more than 10%. (This would imply that world offshore production will more than quadruple in present value by 1990. At present it accounts for about 20% of world oil production.)

Assuming a high growth rate in world oil production for 1975-1990, i.e., 6% per annum, implies a share of 32% for offshore production in 1990. With a lower hypothesis of growth of 3% the offshore share would be 46%.

Results of Inquiry

A questionnaire addressed to a group of energy experts from different countries and professional backgrounds contained two approaches. In the over-all approach, statistical tools were used, to produce over-all results and to group experts according to attitudes. Within each group a representative expert was chosen. In the specific approach, the SMIC method was applied to the questionnaires of the experts chosen, to deduce the scenario and the contrasted scenarios most likely to occur.

Only histograms based on simple probabilities (Fig. 8-1) were drawn up. In general it was found that it is not possible to characterize types by the nationality of the respondents, but their field of activity did influence their answers.

Maintenance of American Leadership

The point is widely admitted. Those who contested it were European (particularly French) or from the Third World. American leadership could be affected somewhat if OPEC solidarity continues, but a breakdown in OPEC would have very diverse effects. There is a link between American leadership and the power of the major oil companies; these two factors reinforce each other. Other factors seem to have little effect. American leadership therefore seems probable over the period and is unlikely to be placed in doubt, whatever happens.

OPEC Solidarity

Opinions are divided, and this is the question on which the experts are most undecided. The spread of opinion shows up in the conditional probabilities. It should be noted that experts from the oil industry in the main believe in the probable maintenance of OPEC cohesion.

The guarantee of investments through a floor price would be unfavorable to OPEC. The nongrowth of reserves would reinforce the prospects of OPEC cohesion, while the converse would tend to promote differences. Some experts consider that a relative abundance of oil outside OPEC countries might lead member countries to seek markets separately, while others think that such a situation might lead, by way of reaction, to a solidifying of OPEC.

Finally it should be noted that the collapse of OPEC, by virtue of the changes it would bring about, is the phenomenon that would most influence the over-all system.

Maintenance of Power by the Major Companies

This point is generally conceded, although among the experts belonging to the oil industry, some are only very moderately "optimistic." American leadership seems likely to play a significant role. OPEC is likely to have little effect, although its disappearance would strengthen the major companies. No particular tendency emerges from the other factors. Only a high rate of growth of offshore activities would increase the probability of this hypothesis.

Increase in Reserves

On this point expert opinion divides into two groups, the pessimists often being from the oil industry. Only the preceding hypothesis would tend to make this hypothesis more plausible.

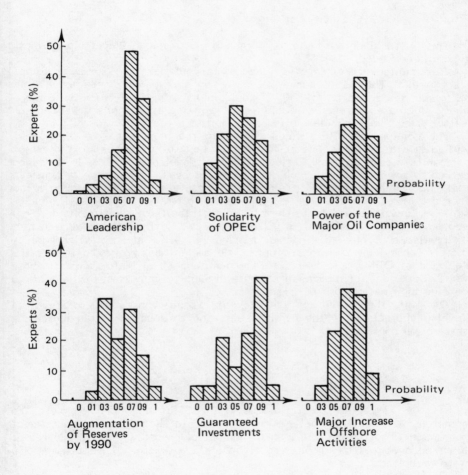

Fig. 8.1. Frequency Histograms of the probabilities accorded by the fundamental hypotheses.

Profitability of Investments

Most of the experts anticipate the maintenance of a floor price over the period, although some do not agree. This is related to the belief of these experts that OPEC has little chance of survival. This would lead to a drop in prices. Increases in reserves, undoubtedly for an analogous reason, would militate against the maintenance of a floor price.

Strong Increase in Offshore Activities

This point, along with the maintenance of American leadership, is most generally conceded.

The maintenance of American leadership would lead the undecided to bet on growth. The maintenance of power by the major companies and in particular the solidarity of OPEC would make a high rate of growth more likely. Increases in reserves would retard growth a little, while the setting of a floor price would stimulate offshore activities perceptibly.

The collapse of OPEC would constitute the most negative factor, but without reversing the general tendency. Loss of influence by the major companies would similarly affect offshore development, but to a minor degree. Views differ on a nonincrease in reserves. Some experts consider that this would stimulate offshore activities; others, that if there is no increase in reserves there is less chance that offshore activities will develop (inverse causal relationship). Unreliable profitability of investments does not appear to deal a fatal blow to offshore prospects. The replies were in fact distributed according to a normal distribution with a mean of 4 (probability 0.5.). Those experts who are optimistic are either those who expect the cohesion of OPEC, and therefore the maintenance of high prices, or those who believe that for reasons of security of supply, many states will decide to develop their national energy resources.

Over-all, the production of offshore hydrocarbons seems destined to develop appreciably in the coming years and to account for an increasing share of oil consumption.

The Processing of the Information

As the 52 replies from experts to the SMIC questionnaire were too numerous for the SMIC method to be applied to each response, an attempt was made to sort them into a small number of groups with a fair degree of likemindedness. (Only replies received at SEMA before 15 February 1976 were evaluated.)

Next, within each group we sought to find the most representative expert. This was the expert who, in all his replies, gave answers representing the majority of the group ("the ideal expert").

To make up these groups, a procedure of hierarchical classification (cluster analysis), which consists of representing the n experts by points in a multidimensional space according to their replies, was used. And to identify

the two individuals closest in terms of their replies to the simple
probabilities, these were replaced by a mean of the two, now considered as a
new individual. This procedure was repeated with the remaining individuals
n-1, and so on.

We were thus led to form 10 groups (the last being an artificial grouping
of experts not fitting into the other nine groups), and to choose 11 experts for
the application of SMIC. By applying this method we were able to classify
the experts into eight relatively homogeneous groups, from which typical
experts were chosen.

The application of SMIC to the replies of these typical experts provided
eight hierarchies of scenarios, each being but one solution among many
possible ones. We had to seek in this diversity of results the median opinion,
or the image of the future that emerged most frequently.

The Choice of Reference and Contrasted Scenarios

The six fundamental hypotheses allowed 2^6 = 64 combinations (i.e., 64
scenarios) of the six events, which will occur or not in the period 1975-1990.

Each scenario was represented schematically by six binary variables 0 or
1 (one per hypothesis), according to whether the corresponding event occurs
or not.

SMIC provides, for each typical expert, the list of the 64 scenarios, each
given an over-all probability of occurrence rating, and ranked in decreasing
order of probability (the sum of these 64 probabilities equaling 1).

In fact for each expert only 15 scenarios had a nonzero probability of
occurrence.

The scenarios chosen by the majority of experts as the most likely were
examined and ranked according to the mean of their probability. This examination allowed the identification of the three most likely lines of development of the geoenergy system starting from the present situation, which can
be written (111000).

Hypotheses		Scenarios		
		A	B	C
H1	American leadership	0	1	1
H2	OPEC solidarity	1	1	0
H3	Major companies	0	1	1
H4	Growth of non-OPEC reserves	0	1	0 or 1
H5	Minimum price	1	1	1
H6	Growth of offshore exploitation	0	1	1

Fig. 8.2

Figure 8-2 illustrates the emergence of a "North/South" reference scenario (hypothesis B) set between two contrasted scenarios, "Scenario South" (hypothesis A) and "Scenario North" (hypothesis C).

In the reference scenario North-South, all six hypotheses would be found realistic in the period 1976-1990. The OPEC countries show a solid front to American power and to that of the major companies. In this context, offshore oil, the minimum price, and the growth of reserves in the non-OPEC zone would be economic and strategic factors of prime importance.

Nevertheless, Western countries remain dependent for their energy on OPEC oil. On the one hand, programs of substitution and exploitation of new reserves encounter substantial technological and financial difficulties, particularly during the period 1976-1980, and, on the other hand, the growth of offshore production also affects the OPEC countries. With oil the basis of power of both actors, there is thus a coincidence of interest between OPEC and the large oil companies, which tends to maintain a prime position for oil in the energy system.

Scenario South would comprise the maintenance of OPEC solidarity, the end of American leadership, and the decline of the major companies. Purely in oil terms, this could be thought of as an "onshore" scenario, since no great increase in offshore activities would be anticipated before the period 1981-1990.

Furthermore, the Western countries would remain very dependent for their energy on OPEC oil, which they would have to pay for dearly, since its price would be fixed in relation to the needs of the Third World's development. The fixing of a floor price of oil, intended to protect the profitability of Western energy investments in case of a drop in OPEC oil prices, would be a hangover from the period 1976 to 1990 and would not serve any purpose since this eventuality would not arise.

Scenario North is characterized by the breakdown of OPEC and the maintenance of American power. There would not necessarily be a great increase in reserves in the non-OPEC zone, but the fixing of a minimum price would allow not only for strategic energy investments to be made during the period 1976 to 1980, but also for the creation of a genuine two-tier energy market in which OPEC oil would be purchased for a price lower than the minimum price applying in the Western zone. Thus the oil revenues would be picked up by the major oil companies and the Western countries.

Nevertheless, the role of offshore oil, exploited particularly in the northern hemisphere, would be increasing, because the Western countries would be anxious to maintain their independence of energy supply, which has cost them dearly and which they almost did not manage to regain.

Conclusion

SMIC allows a preliminary outline to be made of the images of the future that emerge from the various scenarios up to 1990. Once these images have been created, the object of the scenarios method is to describe in a consistent manner the different routes by which these images may be attained.

The function of SMIC can therefore be summarized essentially as identifying the most likely futures to which the scenarios method will be applied.

9 General Conclusion

It is appropriate at this point, not only to bring together all the provisional conclusions drawn from the foregoing, but also to go somewhat beyond the argument presented by reinstating what is of value in classical forecasting, and in speculating about new directions in mathematical forecasting - the works of Prigogine (60) and Thom (61) - and about the future of the prospective approach itself.

SYNTHESIS OF RESULTS

Classical forecasting is typified by a passive or adaptive attitude to the future, in which action and freedom of will (which cannot ultimately be formulated in equations) have no place. On the other hand, the prospective approach restores human action to its rightful place in the process of creating the future. It recognizes the determining role of intentions (the plans of the different actors involved in the systems studied) as a force productive of the future. Allowing for these strategies entails the use of intentional analysis, i.e., all those methods that deal with variables of opinion (judgments, gambles, subjective probabilities) such as structural analysis, cross-impacts, and scenarios.

Prospective methods arose from the awareness that the future is the result of a mixture of determinism and freedom of choice. If we allow that history is forged by human action, then what is determined arises from the past, from crystallized actions; these allow a certain range of possible futures, and not another. Man, however, insofar as he does not overcommit and mortgage his future (very narrow range), retains many degrees of freedom to which he may give play to achieve the potential future he desires.

Thus, the plan produced by wish is the driving force behind action, and therefore change. The past is but an extinct plan, and only the future matters. The future is the raison d'être of the present; "the future explains the present," in the words of C. Goux.

115

Somewhat paradoxically, it is action that makes forecasting necessary, but it is also human action as the basic cause of change which, through the unforeseeable effects of its area of freedom, renders forecasting inadequate. Classical forecasting is impotent to forecast the future according to past data, since what will actually come about depends on the actions man undertakes today to suit the image he creates himself of the future. Repeated forecasting errors, and in particular the absence of forecasts of economic crises, explain what can be called the crisis in forecasting and contribute to the emergence of the prospective.

In order that the prospective should participate in the creation of the future by man, it must be equipped with characteristics radically different from those of classical forecasting to avoid the latter's errors.

We therefore substitute:

- a holistic view for a piecemeal view.

- qualitative and subjective variables and methods for quantitative variables and methods.

- dynamic relationships for static relationships.

- an explanation of the present by the future for an explanation of the future by the past.

- the search for a free and multiple future for the search for a single and predetermined future.

For classical forecasting, we substitute the prospective representing an over-all, qualitative, and multiple forecasting approach.

To obtain an over-all and qualitative view we make use of structural analysis; to gain greater insight into the dynamics of the system we use the MICMAC method. The results should not be taken too literally, but instead should allow, through their counterintuitive aspects, questions to be posed that would not otherwise have been asked.

To obtain a multiple view of an uncertain future, we adopt the method of scenarios, carried out within the logical and methodological framework of an integrated prospective approach in which there is no method without reasoning, or reasoning without method. Method and reasoning serve as cross-checks on each other.

COMPLEMENTARITY BETWEEN PROSPECTIVE AND FORECASTING

To criticize is not to reject, and the chaff must be separated from the wheat. While quantification at any price may seem dangerous, the numerical results of classical forecasting models (mathematical, econometric) do provide stimulating indicators and valuable reference points for a consideration of the future.

As a result when all is said and done, and the debate we would like to see take place has been held, we remain convinced that there is a certain

complementarity between the prospective and classical forecasting. A forecasting model is valuable only by virtue of its hypotheses (economic,
political,...) and the objective of the prospective approach is to paint the
backdrop or set of hypotheses that will provide the model with its validity,
i.e., with its consistency with the future reality such as it may be imagined
and desired.

Naturally, this complementarity is not systematic. In the long term, i.e.
in the time frame in which everything or almost everything may have
changed, the integrated prospective approach places almost no reliance on
classical forecasting methods since structural changes are to be expected.
On the other hand, as the term becomes progressively shorter, classical
methods play an increasingly important role insofar as the continued presence
of certain structural variables can be assumed and trends identified from the
past can be extended without too much misgiving. This is even more the case
- except in periods of profound change - for conjunctural forecasts that rest
on largely proven methods.

NEW DIRECTIONS IN MATHEMATICAL FORECASTING: THE WORKS
OF PRIGOGINE (60) AND THOM (61)

Classical forecasting models are unable to represent and describe an
increasingly complex reality, in which structures are not stable, where
everything acts on everything else, and an over-all view is required. It is just
this taking into account the "societal" interdependencies that marks the use
of systems analysis as a prospective method.

Two schools of systems analysis have developed, almost in parallel. The
first, for which we shall adopt J. Kane's (50) designation of "geometrical,"
argues that not all factors of change are quantifiable. This school therefore
emphasizes the structural analysis of the relationships between variables
characterizing the system, without necessarily specifying the form or content
of these relationships (intensity, function, etc.). The second, which we shall
call "arithmetical," is concerned with the quantitative nature of the relationships and represents the real world by a system of equations (differential
or recurrence). Forrester's "dynamo" model is an example of this second
type.

The disciples of the first school, to which the author feels he belongs,
make use of qualitative mathematical and intellectual tools (structural
analysis, cross-impacts, scenarios method), which we group under the heading
"intentional analysis." This term signifies that the future is not fatalistic, but
largely depends on the plans of the influential actors of a system that, it will
be remembered, is not defined as being reality, but merely a means of
viewing it.

Intentional analysis is proposed as a way of meeting the inadequacy of
classical forecasting models, as reflected in their inability to forecast crises.
Disciples of the "arithmetical" school, however, argue otherwise, attributing
the absence of forecasts of crises, not to the mismodeling of reality, but to
the use of continuous mathematics in order to represent a discontinuous
reality. A new direction was developed involving mathematical forecasting

of ruptures, which R. Thom (61) calls "catastrophe theory" and Prigogine (60) "fluctuation theory" (see Note 1).

Apart from differences of vocabulary, the works of Prigogine and Thom are similar. Both draw upon concepts from the exact sciences, such as physics, thermodynamics (in the realm of physics the transition gas-liquid is a good example of a "catastrophe") and apply them to linguistics, biology, and, currently, social forecasting. These works involve the important presupposition that the world can be fitted into a system of differential equations. Given this point, the mathematical forecasting of ruptures contains an interesting argument, which may be summarized as follows: Reality is represented by a system of differential equations. We know there is only one solution to such a system that passes through a given point in time and space (for example, the present), at least when the boundary conditions are fixed. In the works of Thom and Prigogine, however, the boundary conditions are not fixed; certain environmental parameters exist, which can bring about different possible dynamic regimes, and transition (fluctuation or catastrophe) between these regimes, which make up qualitatively different possible futures.

For certain values of the environmental parameters, there are breaks in evolutionary development, or "catastrophes." Thus, changes in structure occur when "the external disturbance exceeds the capacity to absorb, the social system is destroyed and emerges in a new organization" (Prigogine (60) p. 58). But this catastrophe occurs only if certain external conditions coincide for certain values of the environmental parameters.

Catastrophe theory shows particularly, ex post facto, that the change in structure actually corresponds to a solution of the system of differential equations for a given value of the environmental parameters. However, ex ante, the problem remains of knowing the values of these parameters, and of their evolution, in order to determine whether, among the possible futures, that which will actually come about is a break, a catastrophe, or not.

It is precisely the object of the prospective, taking into account existing forces and the plans of the actors, to determine the values of the environmental parameters, i.e., the trend-based and contrasted scenarios.

In conclusion, independent of the supposition, not endorsed by us, that the world can be represented by a system of differential equations, (unless the system is of almost infinite dimension and therefore unusable or insoluble) the great merit of the work of Prigogine and R. Thom is in allowing account to be taken of structural instability, and to thus open up a new usefulness for mathematical models, which have been released from the impasse of continuous mathematics, and from their inability to envisage a plurality of futures and the possibility of ruptures.

THE FUTURE OF THE PROSPECTIVE APPROACH

The prospective approach, as the creation of the future by man, gives power to the imagination, and in this sense it is revolutionary. In fact, to imagine and construct the path toward a better future, to appreciate that there is nothing impossible, necessarily leads to a great mobilization of forces, activated by desire, to bring it to full fruition.

The prospective approach is therefore not neutral. This is why attempts have been made to assimilate it in cases where the imagination is placed at the service of this or that interest, of this or that ideology, either to detect the germs of a "rupture" in order if possible better to nip it in the bud or at least to limit its effect, or in order to conjure up a specter of the future to better justify present policies.

Thus, for example, it is partly in the name of an alleged future shortage of oil that the nuclear gamble is being justified, but if, as is thought by most experts (Adelman, Grenon, Odell and even those in the oil industry), oil reserves are at least three times greater than official estimates (the concealment is for strategic reasons), what of the nuclear power stations, which will become, if not useless, at least excessively numerous?

In the same way a rather curious panic has been developing since the early 1970s in relation to the year 2000 (see Note 2), sparked off particularly by the famous Meadows reports, the reports of the Club of Rome which, it must be recognized, had the merit of alerting a society resting on its laurels of growth without having necessarily asked the right questions (see Note 3), and in particular of having permitted a certain number of untruths to be transformed into received ideas.

Thus, for example, the world agricultural deficit cannot be explained by the galloping population growth of the countries of the third world, whose imports of cereals in physical terms have been stagnant for fifteen years according to FAO statistics. (This has come about in particular because as the products have become more and more expensive, the poorer countries have been, for the most part, less and less able to pay.) On the contrary, this deficit results from the massive imports the developed countries (including the USSR) for the "transformation" of grain into meat, which without doubt represents a waste of nutritional calories.

This type of speculation about the year 2000 is dangerous insofar as it hides what it does not show; it advances ideas (the exhaustion of natural resources) in order to conceal that behind this there are certain social relationships, a certain international division of wealth. This is the alibi future, the future responsible for present evils. At the same time that an oil shortage is predicted - while we have seen that nothing is less certain - price rises, inflation, etc. are justified, and we rush into technological, ecological, and financial adventures such as nuclear energy without establishing a truly democratic debate.

These predictions and prophecies, insofar as they too often turn out to be contradicted by facts, since they are without foundation, cast discredit on all reflection about the future and devalue the prospective approach, and in consequence the exercise of imagination. In so doing, they weaken the will of the forces of change. Yet the prospective approach has nothing to do with prophecy since it seeks more to ask the right question than to find ready-made answers.

The prospective approach, regarded as a creative method of thinking about the future and about methods of transforming desires and plans into reality, will not pass out of fashion, since man is more and more determined to take the future into his own hands.

As the ideas underlying the prospective approach become more wide-spread - carrying the message that to liberate the future, the present must be liberated from the past, and the political, economic, and social relationships that hold most men in bondage must be broken - so will plans become a material force, and wish will become the main factor in producing the future (see Note 4).

Notes

Chapter 1

(1) In research and development an average of ten years is required to perfect a really new product, and it must therefore be seen in the context of its future market (56).

Chapter 2

(1) With Hegel, dialectics is an apodictic triadic relation: T (thesis) - A (antithesis) - S (synthesis). If Hegel generally avoids these terms, it is obvious that das Dialektische denominates in his philosophy a dynamic structure with three moments. The process T - A - S is, for him, linear or circular, rigorous, univocally determined, and, in the end, nontemporal, as A. Kojève has stressed. The Hegelian dialectics is deterministic in a Laplacian absolutist sense:

$$T - A - S$$

where - indicates a dialectical contradiction or opposition.

With Marx, on the other hand, the dialectical process of T - A - S, as Antonio Gramsci perceived, admits a certain set of syntheses. In fact, it has the following scheme:

$$T\text{-----}A \quad \begin{matrix} S_1 \\ S_2 \\ S_3 \\ \\ \\ S_n \end{matrix}$$

Of course, this scheme is an oversimplified one. T as well as A may be understood as sets of possible and real "opposites," divergent tendencies which involve each other reciprocally.

As such, in Marx's conception, the dialectical process is not a linear but always includes a definite field of possible syntheses with several degrees of probability, depending on conditions.

(2) Subjectivism: In fact we do not admit the schism between knowledge and thought, nor between science and action, nor between the abstract and the concrete. We do not admit separation between that which must be united in a single dialectic (H. Lefebvre) (27, p. 146).

(3) "Hidden variables are an invention; they may not be observed. If they cannot be observed it should be admitted that they have no reality and therefore it may well be that they exist only in the imagination of their authors." (L. Birllouin). Science and Information theory - 2nd edition, New York, 1962 (p. 315).

Chapter 3

(1) The Leontief matrices clearly bring out the structural interdependence between industrial sectors. The rise since 1945 in the ratio of foreign trade over gross national product for most countries illustrates the phenomenon of growing interdependence between economies. Economic forecasting for a given country is thus becoming more and more an analysis of the international economic scene.

(2) "Very often a 'system' cannot be abstracted from its environment without damaging it; it is well known that in quantum mechanics, any observation disturbs a phenomenon in itself, independently of the process of observation". R. Fortet, H. Le Boulanger - Elements for a Synthesis of Self Organising Systems METRA Special Series 22 1967.

Chapter 4

(1) See the works of Benzecri (difficult) and the easier book of Lebart and Fenelon.

(2) See the THOMSON-CSF technical review volume 6 No. 3 September 1974.

Chapter 5

(1) "An event will be considered as random if the only information which we have relating to its past or future realization is incomplete and does not allow us to assert that the event will (occur) or has taken place. To attribute a probability to such an event is to express with the help of a number the whole or a part of the information which one possesses relating to it" (59, p. 6).

(2) "A judgment of probability must be capable of expression in terms of a gamble, and the over-all success of a certain number of gambles is the sole criterion of the validity of the judgment" (Borel) (6, p. 105).

(3) When someone says, "I estimate the probability of such an (isolated) event as 3/4," then we agree with Professor Ville in understanding this judgment as follows: if you noted all the events to which I have attributed a probability of 3/4, and you observed the frequency of those in which the

event actually occurred in a large number of cases, I predict that this frequency will be close to 3/4" (59, p. 17).

(4) "The system formed by the course of events up to the year 2000 and the image of France in this year, built up under the hypothesis that the present trends and activity would continue, would be called a 'trend-based scenario.'" (Underlined in the original) (51, p. 570).

(5) Nevertheless in recent studies we have used the expression "reference scenario" which is intermediate between trend-based and contrasted scenarios.

(6) The computer program achieving this result was developed at the Compagnie Internationale de Services Informatiques by J. Lieutaud from Ravindran's algorithm, Communications of ACM, 1972, Vol. 15, No. 9 (52).

Chapter 8

(1) See 1985 to 1990: Energy and the Role of Nuclear Power. Prospective considerations LCP - CEA December 1973.

(2) In 1965 the target production of CECA (European community for coal and steel) was 330 million tons. The actual production was 250 million tons of coal, or less than the 1953 production.

(3) See World Petroleum Encyclopedia 1975.

(4) Rather curiously since the beginning of the 1970s we have become panic-stricken about the year 2000. The Meadows report in 1972 on the limits of growth, reports of the Club of Rome, etc. tend to show for example that the world agricultural deficit is explained by the population explosion in the Third World, (which is not supported by the Food and Agriculture Organization (F.A.O.) statistics). The panic about the year 2000 is reminiscent of that of "the year 1000." (See the book by George Duby-Julliard, Archives collection).

(5) In France in 1974 the price of gasoline in constant francs was less than it was in 1958 (Le Monde, 29 January 1974).

(6) The strategy of the large American oil companies in the oil crisis is given in Problemes Economiques No. 1363, 1974.

(7) Energy prospects to 1985 OECD Paris 1975.

(8) "The energy crisis and the new world equilibrium 1974-1980". June 1974 GEPI: Groupe d'etudes prospectives internationales of the CFCE: Centre francais du Commerce Extérieur.

(9) 1. "Oil, raw materials and development"

Memorandum presented by Algeria at an extraordinary session of the General Assembly of the United Nations, April 1974.

2. Memorandum presented by Algeria at the Conference of Heads of State of the OPEC countries, March 1975.

(10) See OECD Study.

(11) OECD Study.

(12) GEPI Study page 14.

(13) GEPI Study.

(14) GEPI Forecasts for 1980.

(15) Forecasts for 1980.

(16) This analysis is particularly appropriate for countries such as Algeria, Iran, Indonesia, Nigeria, etc., but does not necessarily square with Saudi Arabia, because of the size of its reserves and of its poor economic potential.

(17) The "turnkey" function would move from the simple provision of factories to greater emphasis on the products of those factories. The vendor is thus rewarded on results: x% of the annual value of the market. If the yield of the factory is poor, or the quality inadequate, the vendor is himself penalized.

(18) See the article by Michel Tatu in Le Monde 9/1/77.

(19) CF. "Oil Trade in 1985," the OECD Observer No. 85, March 1977. The possibility of a deliberate error cannot be ruled out. By presenting optimistic figures, the international bargaining position is strengthened; statistics are not neutral.

Chapter 9

(1) "These are fluctuations which can induce the system to depart from a given macroscopic state and lead to a new state having a different spatio-temporal structure" (60).

(2) This panic regarding the year 2000 recalls that of "the year 1000." See the book of George Duby-Julliard, Archives Collection.

(3) "The world problematique is reduced to an analysis of human and physical resources, and their production and distribution, independently of the social relationships which determine them". G. Ribeill, "A strategy for tomorrow, or utopia without a future?".

(4) It is remarkable that in English the future tense is conveyed by the auxiliary "will," a verb that expresses the human will; the future is intention, plan, desire.

Glossary

OECD, Organization for Economic Cooperation and Development, a consultative body headquartered in Paris and grouping Western countries.

DATAR, Délégation en aménagement des territoires et action rurale. Unit in French Ministry of Interior, concerned with regional development.

CEA, Commissariat a l'énergie atomique. French Atomic Energy Agency.

EDF, Electricité de France. French government-operated power company.

OTAM, Omnium textiles articles ménagers. General trading company.

SEMA-PROSPECTIVE, Paris consulting firm (director: Michel Godet).

GEPI, Groupe d'études prospectives internationales du CFCE (Centre français du Commerce extérieur). Think-tank on energy matters.

MICMAC Matrix of Crossed Impacts. A method of assessing relationships between variables; particularly useful in establishing indirect relationships and feedback between variables.

SMIC Systems and Crossed Impacts Matrix. Discipline designed to subject the judgment of experts on given subjects to a series of constraints with the aim of transforming "raw opinion" into "finished probabilities."

Trend-Based Scenario The construction of a hypothetical future situation on the basis of that course of events which appears most likely at the time the scenario is written.

Contrasting Scenario Scenario based on the exploration of a purposely extreme theme and the a priori determination of a future situation, which, built around such a theme, contrasts strongly with the present and any scenario based on currently prevailing trends.

Bibliography

(1) Samir, A. 1971. L'accumulation à l'échelle mondiale. 2nd ed. Paris: Anthropos.

(2) Apostol, P. 1972. Marxism and the structure of the future. Futures 4, no. 3 (September): 201-210.

(3) Bachelard, G. 1970. La formation de l'esprit scientifique. 7th ed. Paris: Librairie philosophique, J. Urin.

(4) Barel, Y. 1971. Prospective et analyse de système. Paris: Documentation française.

(5) Bartoli, H. 1958. Note sur le déterminisme et l'indéterminisme en économie. Cahiers de l'ISEA no. 3, ser. M, pp. 69-88.

(6) Berger, G. 1967. Etapes de la prospective. Paris: Presses Universitaires de France.

(7) Berger, G. 1964. Phénoménologie du temps et prospective. Paris: Presses Universitaires de France.

(8) Boudon, R. 1970. L'analyse mathématique des faits sociaux. 2nd ed. Paris: Plon.

(9) Breton, A. 1967. Les vases communicants. Paris: Gallimard.

(10) Broglie, L. 1937. Réflexions sur l'indéterminisme en physique quantique. Travaux du IX Congrès International de Philosophie. Paris: Hermann.

(11) Camus, A. 1965. Le mythe de Sisyphe. Paris: Gallimard (la Pléiade).

(12) Chombart de Lauwe, P.H. 1970. Aspirations et transformations sociales. Paris: Anthropos.

(13) Delattre, P. 1971. Système, structure, fonction, évolution. Paris: Maloine Doin.

(14) Denis, H. 1966. Histoire de la pensée economique. Paris: Presses Universitaires de France.

(15) Romeuf, J. 1958. Dictionnaire des sciences économiques. Paris: Presses Universitaires de France.

(16) Friedman, M. 1957. A theory of the consumption function. Princeton, N.J.: Princeton University Press.

(17) Goldmann, L. 1969. Logique et connaissance scientifique. Paris: Gallimard (la Pléiade).

(18) Goldmann, L. 1970. Marxisme et sciences humaines. Paris: Gallimard (idées).

(19) Goux, C. 1969. L'horizon prévisionnel. Paris: Cujas.

(20) Goux, C. et Morel, B. 1971. Pour une véritable prospective: essai méthodologique. Metra X, no. 3: 339-352.

(21) Gordon, W.J.J. 1965. Stimulation des facultés créatrices. Paris: Hommes et Techniques.

(22) Grimaldi, N. 1971. Le désir et le temps. Paris: Presses Universitaires de France.

(23) Illich, I. 1972. Inverser les institutions. Esprit, no. 3 (March), pp. 321-367.

(24) Jouvenel, B. 1964. L'art de la conjecture. Monaco: Du Rocher.

(25) Keynes, J.M. 1969. Théorie générale de l'emploi, de l'intérêt et de la monnaie. Paris: Payot.

(26) Korganoff et Pavel Parvu. 1967 Méthodes de calcul numérique. Paris: Gauthier-Villars.

(27) Lefebvre, M. 1968. La vie quotidienne dans le monde moderne. Paris: Gallimard.

(28) Levi-Strauss, 1962. La pensée sauvage. Paris: Plon.

(29) Macrae, N. 1972. The future of international business. The Economist (January 22).

(30) Marx, K. 1963. Ctitique de l'économie politique - Oeuvres - Economie I. Paris: N.R. La Pléiade.

(31) Mendel, E. 1970. La formation de la pensée économique de Karl Marx. Paris: Maspero.

(32) Mesavoric, M.D. 1964. Views on general system theory. New York: Wiley.

(33) Morgenstern, O. 1972. Précision et incertitudes des données économiques. Paris: Dunod.

(34) Morgenstern, O. 1971. L'économie est-elle une science exacte. La Recherche 2, no. 18 (December): 1023-1028.

(35) Ponsard, C. 1973. L'imprécision et son traitement en analyse économique. Memo, IME, University of Dijon (September).

(36) Ribeill, G. 1972. Systèmes: analyse et théorie - système et formation. Memo, DS, Metra no. 55 (May).

(37) Villey, D. et Neme, C. 1973. Petite histoire des grandes doctrines économiques. 2nd ed. Paris: Genin.

(38) Ayres, R.U. 1972. Prévision technologique et planification a long terme. Paris: Hommes et Techniques.

(39) Bluet, J.C. et Zemor, J. 1970. Prospective géographique, méthode et direction de recherche. Metra IX, no. 1: 111-127.

(40) Borel, E. 1949. Eléments de la théorie des probabilités. Paris: Albin-Michel.

(41) Dalkey, M. 1972. An elementary cross impact model. Technological forecasting and social change 3, no. 3: 341-351.

(42) DATAR (délégation à l'aménagement du territoire et à l'action régionale). 1971. Un scénario de l'inacceptable. Paris: Documentation Francaise, collection TRP.

(43) Duval, A., Fontela, E. et Gabus, A. 1974. Cross impact. A handbook on concepts and applications. Memo, Batelle (Dematel reports no. 1), Genève, p. 76.

(44) Eymard, J. 1977. A Markovian cross impact model. Futures 9, no. 3 (June): 216-228.

(45) Florentin, J.P. et Isaac-Dognin, J.M. 1973. Utilisation de l'analyse d'interaction. Thesis, University of Dauphine, Paris (June).

(46) Fontela, E. et Gabus, A. 1974. Events and economic forecasting models. Futures 6, no. 4 (August): 329-333.

(47) Gordon, T.J. 1968. Initial experiment with the cross impact matrix method of forecasting. Futures 1, no. 2 (December): 100-116.

(48) Howard et Johnson. 1970. Some computational aspects of cross impacts matrix forecasting. Futures 2, no. 2 (June): 123-131.

(49) Jantsch, E. 1967. La prévision technologique. Paris: OECD.

(50) Kane, J. 1972. A primer for a new cross impact language K.S.I.M. Technological forecasting and social change 4, no. 2: 129-142.

(51) Landrieu-Zemor, J. Une méthode d'analyse prospective, son élaboration dans le cadre du scénario tendanciel français. Metra X, no. 4: 569-626.

(52) Lieutaud, M. 1974. SMIC program d'après un algorithme de Ravindran, communications of the ACM, vol. 15, Nov. 1972. Memo Commissariat à l'Energie Atomique.

(53) McLean, J.M., Shepherd et Curnon, R.C. 1974. An empirical investigation into systematics, the study of behaviour of large complex systems. Memo, University of Sussex (S.P.R.U.) (November).

(54) Maestre, C. 1973. Analyse du système scientifique national. Symposium on system analysis communications, OECD (October 22-24).

Michel, J. 1973. Analyse structurelle et la définition de la recherche en matière d'habitat. Symposium on system analysis communications, OECD (October 22-24).

Lemieux, V. 1973. Analyse des relations de puissance. Symposium on system analysis communications, OECD (October 22-24).

(55) Roberts, P. Pulse processes on signed digraphs: a tool for analysing energy demand. NSF, nos. 5926, 5927 (March/April).

(56) Saint-Paul, R. et Teniere Buchot, P.F. 1974. Innovation et évaluation technologique. Paris: Entreprise Moderne d'Edition.

(57) Teniere-Buchot, P.F. 1973. Modèle Popole. Analyse et Prévision, SEDES 15 (February/March).

(58) Tiano, A. 1974. La méthode prospective. Paris: Dunod.

(59) Ville, J. 1937. Etude critique de la notion de collectif. Paris: Gauthier-Villars.

(60) Prigogine, I. et Glansdroff, P. 1977. Structure, stabilité et fluctuations. Paris: Masson.

(61) Thom, R. 1972. Stabilité structurelle et morphogenèse. Essai d'une théorie générale des modèles. Paris: Ediscience.

(62) Duperrin, J.C. et Godet, M. 1973. Méthode de hiérarchisation des éléments d'un système. Rapport économique, C.E.A. R.4541 (December).

(63) Duperrin, J.C. et Godet, M. 1975. SMIC 74: a new cross impact method. Futures 7, no. 4 (August): 302, 312.

(64) Duperrin, J.C., Godet, M. et Puiseux, L. 1975. Les scénarios du développement de l'énergie nucléaire à l'horizon 2000. Rapport économique, CEA R.4684 (July).

(65) Godet, M. 1976. Scenarios of air transport development to 1990 by SMIC 74 a new cross impact method. Technological forecasting and social change 9: 279-288.

(66) Mitchell et Tydeman. 1976. A note on SMIC 74. Futures 3, no. 1 (February): 64-67.

(67) Godet, M. 1974. Prospective des systèmes. Thesis, Faculty of Sciences, Paris VI.

(68) Godet, M. 1976. SMIC, a reply from the authors. Futures 8, no. 4 (August): 336-340.

(69) Lefebvre, J.F. 1975. Une méthode d'analyse structurelle. Metra XIV, no. 4: 635-659.

(70) Durand, R. 1975. Delphi et prospective de l'hydrogène. Metra XIV, no. 4: 617-633.

Index

About the Author

MICHEL GODET, author of "The Crisis in Forecasting and the Emergence of the Prospective Approach" was born in France, holds doctorates in economics and science, and is a lecturer at Lille University. Dr. Godet was the director of SEMA--PROSPECTIVE, which forms part of METRA, the largest European consulting group, until the end of 1978. He currently is with the Commission of the European Community, Brussels.

PHILIPPE DE SEYNES, who wrote the foreword, held a number of high civil service and diplomatic posts in the French government and is a former Under-Secretary-General of the United Nations. He is now a Senior Special Fellow at the United Nations Institute for Training and Research, and Director of the Special Project on the Future. He is also a consultant to the Secretary-General of the United Nations.

Pergamon Policy Studies